Women Poets: Crossing the Boundaries
Volume I

(An Initiative of Progressive Literary & Cultural Society)

Women Poets: Crossing the Boundaries
Volume I

(An Initiative of Progressive Literary & Cultural Society)

Editors

Shamenaz

Lucilla Trapazzo

Kanu Priya Verma

Self Published in 2021 by Notionpress, India
E-mail: plcs.23aug@gmail.com

Women Poets : Crossing the Boundaries (An Anthology of Poems by Women Poets) Volume I
Copyright © 2021 Editors & Poets
ISBN - 9798885463041

Cover Design: Shamenaz
Cover Pic: Manju Yadav

Content

i) Lavender

27. Debra Mascarenhas (UAE)

i) Miss You

ii) Mystery of Missing Girl

28. Zaneta Johns (USA)

i) Not Her Fault

ii) No Footprints

29. Bridie Breen (UK)

i) Timeout

ii)Wonder of Life

30. Jill Sharon Kimmelman (USA)

i) A Woman's Prayer

ii) Missing Your Poet's Voice

Preface

Women Poets: Crossing the Boundaries Volume I is the Fourth book by the Editorial team of Progressive Literary & Cultural Society, a forum which is committed to promote global literature and culture. The motto of PLCS is "Entire Universe is Our Family " which is taken from the Sanskrit word, "Vasudhaiva Kutumbakam". The aim of PLCS is to promote the indegenous literature and culture of almost all the countries of the world. Its mission is to enhance peace, love, multiculturalism, mutual understanding and brotherhood among different nationalities and its vision is to make this world a multicultural hub without any prejudices.

PLCS has organized many poetry readings in the past including Women Poetry Readings. This book is the outcome of the event, "Women Poets: Crossing the Boundaries" organized on 8th August 2021 in which Lucilla Trapazzo (PLCS Italian Coordinator) acted as Convenor and Dr. Kanu Priya Verma (PLCS Indian Coordinator) acted as Co-Convenor. The event showcased the poetry recitation of 23 women poets belonging to 19 countries and 5 continents. Countries including; India, Switzerland, Italy, USA, Greece, Turkey, Spain, Albania,

Croatia, Indonesia, Philippines, South Africa, Chile, Macedonia Morocco, UAE and U. K. participated.

Participating poets include; Shamenaz, Kanu Priya Verma, Lucilla Trapazzo, Sabrina De Canio, Annette Tarpley, Reema Sharma Smaragdi Mitropoulou, Ranjana Sharan Sinha, Muhsine Arda, Manju Yadav, Nalini Tandon (India/USA), Kimberley Crafton, Erina Coku, Alka Prakash, Iva Santini, Purwanti Kusumaningtyas, Anna Maria Dall'Olio, Helen Sarita, Neerja Sachdev, Manisha Singh, Glória Sofia, Amelia Cayul Tranamil and Dalila Hiaoui.

This is an initiative of PLCS to encourage women poets to demonstrate their talents on international front.

Shamenaz
Author/Editor & Translator
of 26 Books
President - PLCS

In the Line of the Mothers

In a male-centered culture, for centuries women have surrendered to silence and have been placed outside the frame of official culture, limited to their roles as mothers and caregivers. The preponderance of art made by males is a given fact. Until the 1960s, women to succeed had to "toughen up," to de-gender and refuse the innate feminine. It is not before the 1990s that a new generation of female artists and literates re-discovered the unswerving vocalization of difference in gender, thus celebrating the display of the feminine as an art language (ignored before or considered minor).

Women are half the world, and being also mothers, who give birth, nourish and raise children, they shape the next generation. Yet despite all, women are routinely discriminated against within and outside their homes, all over the world. In many Countries they are still educated less carefully and not encouraged to excel as much as their male siblings and friends, and discouraged from daring to dream high in the professional life.

The UN, in the early 1990's, created the Human Development Index (HDI) with the explicit purpose *"to shift the focus of development economics from national income accounting to people-centered policies"*. The question of women's wellbeing is central to the economy of every Country. As long as the development index for men and women is unequal, a society cannot be labeled as fully developed, no matter how high its national income. Low levels of human and gender development still characterize many nations, and the results are poverty, malnutrition, inequality, and illiteracy. The importance of investing in human resources via education, especially of women, holds the key to human progress; it also helps push economic growth of a Nation to the next level. Empowering women requires an all-around effort from childhood onwards.

Much has been done in the last hundred years for the recognition of women's rights and voices, thanks to the action of individuals or of feminist movements, but much remains to be done so that women can truly enjoy opportunities equal to those of men. I am convinced that only culture can defeat the ignorance and prejudice that are at the origin of so many abuses of which women are still victims.

I am deeply grateful to PLCS for accepting with enthusiasm my proposal of a poetic event gathering a hand-picked group of women, poets from different parts of the World, whose voices are strong, luminous, free, and also moments of revelation of an intimate space, but mostly, deeply human. Asserting one's own voice also means becoming semiotic vehicles creating another reality, a bridge between the mundane and the private. This is the *fill-rouge* that connects our women-poets, with their indomitable voices they are catalyzing the discovery of a world far too long hidden, that of female interaction and artistic creation, with its rituals and language, often not legitimized (I am thinking of narrative and artistic forms such as embroidery, sewing, collective storytelling, fairy tales, lullabies). Throughout the history of the last three thousand years, women have too often made only private use of their verbal and intellectual talents; around fires, in bathrooms, in kitchens, in living rooms, it is only among them that women have been free to narrate and manifest emotions, not only the "gentle" ones such as love, sweetness, but also the screams, the pain, the sensual. Gender studies show how the female artistic language of the last decades is often an attempt to rediscover the ancient tradition of oral storytelling. The feminine sphere is the first channel of communication, of transmission of knowledge, of signs, of meaning, that we experience. This dimension we want to discover, embrace and manifest, with intimate and strong verses, made of words-signs, of sense and feeling, beyond the referential content.

Women's voice has been silenced and we must uncover it, also by connecting with the soul and the values of the feminine. It is a matrilineal line that runs throughout all history, parallel and intertwining with the matrilineal one. We are not here to argue for reverse discrimination, but to hear the voices of all human beings, irrespective of their gender identification, who are oppressed and marginalized.

We are here as women, as artists, mothers, sisters, poets. We are here to inspire and support.

Lucilla Trapazzo
Italian Poet & Translator

Shamenaz

Dr Shamenaz is the Author, Co-Author, Editor and Translator of 26 international books which includes short stories collections, poetry anthologies, literary articles, criticism & travelogue. Her latest book is an international project of International Multilingual Network, Azerbaijan, *Prism: A Multilingual Anthology*. Being a prolific writer, she holds a D.Phil. in English Literature from University of Allahabad, India with a specialization in South Asian Writers, and New Literature. She is an orator and has been invited by many national and international Colleges & Universities to deliver lectures. She has published poems in many international magazines and journals around the globe. She is currently teaching English Literature at Rajarshi Tandon Mahila Mahavidhyalaya, Allahabad since 2018. She has taught English Literature and Language at S. S. Khanna Girls' Degree College, Ewing Christian College, Allahabad University and Communication Skills at Allahabad Institute of Engineering & Technology. She has professional experience for more than 18 years.

She has published 75 research papers in National & International journals across the globe and has presented papers in 55 National & Seminars/Conferences all over India. She is a member of the Editorial Board of many international journals, including Angloamericanae Journal (Macedonia), KJHSS

(Azerbaijan) *Anglisticum* (Macedonia), *IJRHS* (Jordan), *Cyber Literature: An Online Journal, The Context, English Literator Society, Literary Miscellany, Research Access & Expressions, Levure Litteraire* (France-Germany-USA). She is also the Board of Director of Wildfire Magazine, USA.

She is the Founder & President of Progressive Literary & Cultural Society, an international organization for the promotion of global literature & culture and has successfully organized Golden Words Uzbek Virtual Poetry Festival on 19th and 20th December 2020.

Yes I Am a Sinner

Yes, I am a sinner,

because I am a woman,

my birth is my crime,

and my punishment is life-long slavery,

which I have to bear throughout my life.

If I speak, it is a sin

If I laugh, it is a sin

If I cross four walls of my house, it is a sin

If I put make-up, it is a sin

If I wear short dress, it is a sin

If I roam alone, it is a sin

If I don't lower my gaze, it is a sin.

This society sets parameter of my life,

the measurement of my happiness,

the boundaries of my desires,

the limitations of my rights,

the confinement of my personality,

the length of my skirt.

If, I keep desire, it is a sin

If I move forward, it is a sin

If I fight against atrocities, it is a sin

If I raise my voice, it is a sin

If I break conventions, it is a sin

If I cross the boundaries, it is a sin

When will this society grant me my real freedom?

Women is the Synonym of Strength

Women is the Synonym of Strength

Power, force and glory

residing in various relationships

and various forms on this earth.

She is like flower water,

pure in every aspects

Has ability to absorb

all kinds of impurities of life,

existing in any way.

She is tender, calm and serene

in fullest measure,

has ability to adjust

in any situations and conditions,

no matter how tough and challenging it is.

But when she is in fierce form,

has the capacity to bring the worst destruction.

Lucilla Trapazzo

Lucilla Trapazzo is an Italian residing in Switzerland. She
is an award-winning, internationally recognized
poet, translator, book editor, artist and performer. She is the
Poetry editor of *Mock Up* Magazine (Italy) and Editorial Board
member of INNSAEI Journal, India, juror of poetry
competitions, moderator and co-organizer of international
festivals and art exhibitions. Her works have been translated
into 14 languages, published in international anthologies and
literary magazines. Guest of International Festivals – North
Macedonia (including *Struga Poetry Evenings*), Tunisia,
Albania, Serbia, Italy, Argentina, Columbia, Croatia, India,
Crimea, China, her poems have been awarded numerous prizes
Her books include;

"Ossidiana", poetry book, September 2018, Volturnia
Edizioni, Isernia, Italy.

"Dei Piccoli Mondi", poetry book, April 2019, Il Leggio
Edizioni, Chioggia, Venezia.

"Trentagiorni", Haiku Lucilla Trapazzo, fotografie Alfio
Sacco, September 2019, Il Sextante, Roma.

"Ruscellante", poetry, April 2019, Volturnia Edizioni, Cerro al
Volturno, IS, Italy.

Co-editor, *"Nellostesso Mare"*, Tunisian-Italian poetry anthology, Tunisia, 2020.

Co-editor and translator, *"TransitiPoetici – Voci dal Mondo"*, International poetry anthology, Italy, 2020.

Co-editor and co-author, *"Transitipoeticiincontrail GAP"*, CircoloLetterarioAnastasiano, 2021.

Co-editor, *"Golden Words"*, Multilingual Poetry Anthology, Progressive Literary & Cultural Society, India-Uzbekistan, 2021.

CD –featured in Marco Di Stefano's CD, *Multiverse*, Blue Spiral Records, composed on six of her poems, 202

Jenny Lineage

I beg your pardon; I have no signs to give
May I perhaps surprise you with a gesture?
I don't know, maybe knotting my silk scarf
around your neck.

- Wait! Tell me. Do you own the yarn of the labyrinth?
Have you ever heard the voice of the placenta?
Right when it falls, when out of nothing a sound
is born.

- Stay and listen to me. After all, we are children of the
same mother.
Please stay! And sing me the secret of the tree
of its bark, and then of the sky
the blood.

- Excuse me again. Don't let these seeds get lost to the
wind.
We will be in the forest again, do you know? Earth
and cherry blossoms, in the world we will be present
eternal

tiny blades of grass. And once we'll no longer be
we will – perhaps - realize
the infinite.

Ballad for a Woman

Get up woman, and brandish a rose

you are sister, you are bread, and you are bride.

When thorns are greedy and piercing your flesh,

when drops of blood and of pain are flooding

your breast of butter is ready for mercy.

Under your skirt nectar and torment

close your eyes and you won't feel anything.

Fly higher than a snowy white mountain

your freedom lives in a dream never dreamt!

Kanu Priya Verma

Dr. Kanu Priya Verma is currently working as an Assistant Professor in the Department of Applied Sciences & Humanities, Institute of Engineering & Technology, Dr. Shakuntala Mishra National Rehabilitation University, Lucknow. She has completed her graduation, post graduation and D.Phil degree from University of Allahabad, Prayagraj. She has been actively engaged in teaching and evaluation in her institution. She teaches English, Language and Literature Under-graduate students.

Dr. Verma is a poet and creative writer who has many articles published in different journals and books across the country. She has organized UGC sponsored national seminars, personality development and creative writing workshops in her teaching career. She was NSS coordinator and member of Women Grievance Cell in ISDC, Prayagraj. She has been an academic coordinator and has co-convenored "Technical Fest" in the institute.

Silence

Hush hush…

Here it comes…

There it goes…

And then the silence…

Can I still feel your heart

Bleeding drop by drop

Into that ocean of love.

This soundless silence is your choice

You utter but can't raise your voice

Words have been stolen from your lips

Like life devoid of bliss

Wind is blowing

Your solitude is growing

Stars in the night

Full of bright light

Your heart is at its flight

I can still feel the sight

Don't know why one becomes so speechless
Truth on the lips but wordless

Murmur, whisper in the eerie night
Where love is at its plight

Is silence strength or fate?
Don't know till when to wait…

Hush hush…
Here it comes…
There it goes..

And then the silence.

Is She a Duffer?

Is she a duffer

Is she a fool

Or is she befooled.

Why is she demeaned?

Why is she mocked?

Why is she belittled?

What is her fault?

Why is she to be blamed?

Always be defamed

Things to be done by force

Or task against wish need to be accomplished

Condemned outright, lips tight.

Is she fragile?

Is she docile?

She can be derided.

Is it because she is she

Who cannot flee?

From the fragments of history

Is she doomed to bear the scars?

Be an underdog of male chauvinism

Cave into bed

Voluptuous to tread

Is she a duffer, fool or befooled ?

Sabrina De Canio

Sabrina De Canio (Piacenza, Italy) is an award-winning internationally-acknowledged poet, Literature teacher, translator and co-director of Saint Christopher's Poetry Museum, the only one of its kind in the world. Years spent in Africa gave rise to her underlying theme, namely, resistance to adversity. Her 'Libera Nos a Malo' was published in 2020.

Marbles

The sloping hull

fills with noise

astonished bodies, embraced

roll like marbles

releasing the keel.

Stop shouting

Silence

I want to listen

sunset's and night's secrets

the frizzing foam

the teeth of the parrot fish

gnawing coral

the ticking of the hermit crab on the shore

when water is still hot

at the ankles

and ray hides in the sand.

Is this the sea

transparent up to the roots

where mermaids graze

and desert's fishermen swim

in apnea

with long colorful skirts

faster than a flash

grabbing treasures for lunch

of noisy slow boats

in plates of warm and tasty bread?

I fell asleep

in this dream mom

after following curious dolphins

and sparkling fish

like torches in the night

but now

at the bottom of the blue I am cold

I no longer feel my hand in yours.

I listen to the big trees of the highlands

praying

while I'm looking for you.

Annette Tarpley

Annette Tarpley is a poet from the United States, who has been writing prolifically for the last year and is known internationally. She has published two books, Poetry and Potpourri and Two Hearts, and is the founder and administrator of The Passion of Poetry Facebook site, and is working on her third book an anthology for the site, which will contain Poems from over 100 people, the site now boasts 10 K members.

There is Hope in Tomorrow...

As I think about tomorrow, with all of its possibilities
I think about a world, where mankind embraces humility

I think about a healthy planet, free from all ailments and
disease
A glorious atmosphere of acceptance…disgruntled natures
cease

Tomorrow is a new beginning, where our children can thrive
and grow
For we have instilled within them, the valuable insight that we
know

Tomorrow is our future; we have relinquished the mistakes of
our past
Together, let us make the best of our days, for our time is
fading fast

We have only one journey to travel; on the planet we call earth
Cast aside hostilities, let love guide us to a welcomed rebirth

Let joy and harmony, give our lives a sense of purposefulness
So that our tomorrow can be filled, with contentment and
happiness

Although life can weigh us down, and we may find it hard to cope
Tomorrow promises a new day, bestowing a gift for love and hope

The Beauty and the Butterfly

There was a young beauty, she lived in the woods
Beyond beauty, wisdom she lacked…she did what she could

Her long blond hair cascaded and flowed in the breeze
It seemed to allure the men, flaunting it would tease

Her eyes the color of sapphires, memorized both man and beast
Overall, her visage was lovely, eye candy…she was a feast

She cared not what she looked like, gaining wisdom she did
seek
She knew not how to attain it; she was rather withdrawn and
meek

Avoiding the attentions of onlookers, in the woods she
frolicked at night
She was all alone with nature, satiated by stars and the moon so
bright

A lovely soprano voice she possessed and lyrics would escape
her lips
One night something caught her eye that would change future
trips

A bright and glowing butterfly, fluttered near her and caught
her eye

She was startled and afraid for it spoke; puzzled…she stifled a
cry

Be not afraid dear one, I am here to instill you with wisdom…
you'll become wise
They would meet often, and became friends…what an uncanny
surprise

Lessons the glowing butterfly taught, of note, on harmony,
love, and peace
In her life she began to share her knowledge, of these lessons
she would preach

People looked at her differently, she now had knowledge, and
respect she did find
It is said, she could be heard at night singing, with something
that fluttered and shined

©Annette (Wengert) Tarpley

Reema Sharma

She is working as Assistant Professor in IASE BILASPUR.

She writes poems in English and Hindi.

The Change is Good

I remember the days

not long back

when we met the friends

to live the life

hugged each other

to assure we are living

meetings and eating

where the symbol of life

the doors were always opened

 to welcome the ray of life inside

with the sense of happiness

and belongingness

but the days have changed

and so has life

now I keep away from my friends

so that they can live

I have abandoned myself

so that I can live

the doors are closed

to let the life live,

I wonder has the life has changed?

yes it has, but for good

after so many years of

yarning and wandering

and hiding myself

behind my friends ,

I feel I have suddenly broken those bars ,

cleaned the shadow and met with myself,

the real me , with no covers and an honest smile

I feel that the closed doors

have made me free,

free from the worldly life

free from pretending to be happy

when I really am not,

I remember

my mother used to say

whatever happens for good

and though it is tiring at times

I do feel this change is good

this change is for good

at least I don't have to mask my thoughts,

it is only my face that I mask

so this change is good

this change is really good.

An analysis of I

It's me it's my it's I, and I

and that is the cry

everywhere

we think its Glory

it's the same old story

leaving passages divine

it's I ,me, mine

when I say with pride

I am free of this tide

there is someone

in the corner of my heart

who asks a lot

why do I feel cheated

when someone says no

why I want people to

listen to me and go,

why do I feel bad

when I am criticized

why is that,

that in spite of the thought

which makes me say

I am not of that lot

I feel left out when people

ignore and go

why does it happen

that I feel that life

should begin and end with me

why can't I shed out the mask

why it looks like a difficult task

to free myself from me

when somebody asks

 that question inside me

why is this mess

I stand in the corner

dumbfounded all amiss

to tell you the truth

I don't have an answer to this.

try as I might

I don't have answer to this

Smaragdi Mitropoulou

Smaragdi Mitropoulou was born in Athens. She has studied history and archeology at the University of Athens and had postgraduate history studies at the University of Cardiff, in Great Britain. She serves in secondary education. She is also a Creative Writing graduate (Diploma in Creative Writing) from the Writers' Bureau College (Manchester, UK), and has studied theater writing at the International Theater Institute and directing at the Foundation of Culture in Tinos Island. She has received awards in Greece and abroad for her poetry and prose. Also, she is Programme Coordinator of Writers Capital International Foundation and Greek Representative of Progressive Literary and Cultural Society. So far, she has written five books, which have been published and launched in Greece. Two of them, "One moment just an eternity" and "Sounds in the Silence" have been translated into English and were published in 2020 and 2021.

Eternity

Dressed in a white tunic

 sunbeams embroidered

and bare feet

 along the river I walk.

Dressed in a golden tunic

above the stars I rose.

Dressed in a red tunic

I tasted passion over the centuries.

With you

in the circle of heaven

in the circle of sea

in the circle of earth.

With you

in the walls of war

in the whisper of peace

in the blonde cornfields.

With you

in the sounds of music

in the homelands we loved

yesterday, today, tomorrow,

forever.

With you

on the pages engraved inside us

in the light, in the dark

in the miracle of life.

 History

Now begins.

To My Beloved

Your eyes oh my beloved

 are clearer than the waters of Nile River

your lips redder than the flowers of the sacred lake

your embrace more vast than the desert.

Let me touch

your golden sandals

let me slowly raise my eyes

to face your celestial gaze.

If your hand even fleetingly

touches my hand

If your lips

touch my forehead

 I will be the happiest among mortals!

Open oh gates of Basted Temple open

it's the night of the full moon…

open oh gates of Basted Temple open

what I love most   in front of me to see…

Ranjana Sharan Sinha

Dr. Ranjana Sharan Sinha is a famous poet/author and is a well-known voice in Indian Poetry in English with international recognition. She is a retired professor of English and presently research supervisor (English), RTM Nagpur University, Nagpur, India. She has the honour of receiving a number of awards for her contribution to literature including a commendation from the former President of India, A.P.J. Abdul Kalam for her poem 'Mother Nature'. She has received many national and international awards.

Her poems have been included in the syllabus prescribed for M.A.(English), Purnea University, Purnia. Her poems have been widely published at national and international levels in highly- acclaimed dailies, magazines, e-zines, archives and journals both in print and online including SahityaAkademi's Journal Indian Literature. Her poems have appeared in more than 42 international anthologies like Atunis Galaktika, Inner Child Press, USA, Kali Project, Indie Blu(e) Publishers, USA, Poet, UK, Our Poetry Archive, International Sufi Anthology, Bangalore and many more. Her poems have been translated and published into German, Spanish, Albanian, Greek, Russian, Persian, Nepali and Hindi languages. She has authored and published 09 books in different genres in English and 50 research papers: 1. Spring Zone' (A collection of poems and

Haiku) 2. Midnight Sun (A collection of short stories) 3. Nature in the Poetry of William Wordsworth and Sumitra Nandan Pant.(A comparative critical study) 4. Feminism: Times and Tides (A historiographical and theoretical commentary on Feminism) 5. Different Dimensions (A compilation of research papers presented in various national and international conferences and seminars) 6. Scents and Shadows (A collection of poems) 7. Rhymes for Children (Nursery Rhymes) 8. The Purple Jacaranda and Other Poems (A collection of Poems) 9. Ek Sita Main Bhee (A collection of poems in Hindi). She has completed and published a UGC- approved MRP on comparative literature. Dr. Sharan is associated with many global literary organizations/forums and Poetry Groups. One of the moderators of Pentasi B Poetry and a member of the Editorial Board, Our Poetry Archive.

Pegasus on the Wing

Ooh, the power and puissance of magic,
Beyond the dry and cold touch of logic!

Soaring over the roaring oceans,
In a flight full of amazing motions!

Overlooking the vast fields of white lilies:
Lovesome and pure like lissome lassies!

Reaching distant lands yet unexplored,
A creature that the Greek gods adored!

Beyond the boundaries of time and space,
A symbol of ultimate freedom and grace.

Yes, you're Pegasus, the winged stallion:
A marvel of creation and real inspiration:

The great horse of Greek mythology,
Expressed in wonderful poetic eulogy!

Make me fly in the boundless blue sky
On your wings of love -- high quite high!

Lift me above perceived limitations
To a region without dull stagnations:

Miraculous caves of my imaginations

Pulsating with hypnotic reverberations!

A wish to catch the alluring moon
Hanging like a big bright balloon

Amid incandescent silver stars
And splendour of constellations!

A City of Strangers

A Janus- faced city
Under a blue- black vault,
The burnt- out ends of
A million smoky days
Seem to conspire to a wasteland
Ravaged by uncertainties and solitude.

Life without a heartbeat:
The rush and tumble amid
The mask- wearing robots!
Love --- strings of blinking bulbs--
Gropes through the mist
Soused with darkness,
Like the images drawn up
On fogged up windows.

Unbelievable play of paradoxes --
Extreme noise... extreme silence!
Laughing through tears,
Crying through smiles,
Crazy faces with chaotic feet --
Where do they go?

From the city space to the moon,

And the canvas of stars,

The uplands hang like

A trackless wilderness,

Without babbling Brooks of life;

Some feverish dreams caught

In the web of constellation;

All's changed since I,

Playing with the childhood friends

In this city, once intimate,

Enjoyed many blissful moments!

Oh, some elusive innocent shadows

Come with a scent sublime

Touching every fiber of my being!

A quantum leap in imagination --

The heart trembles in anticipation;

Surprise rainstorms shower the dry zone--

Spring suddenly sweeps:

Brilliant desert flowers bloom

To blanket the arid land!

Muhsine Arda

Muhsine Arda is a Turkish poet, novelist and essayist. A staunch advocate of Women's Rights, her feminist viewpoint is reflected in much of her writing. Till date she has published books in all genre; novel, short stories, poetry anthologies and prose.

The Cry of a Soul

I Am a Stone-Hearted Mother

My husband, my dearest,
God rest his soul
Was very young, my man
Finished by tuberculosis

I was left
In a helpless state
With two kids tugging at my skirt

She doesn't know how lucky she is
The widow forced to marry her brother-in-law

Instead luck knocked on my door with the hand of my father-in-law
"Don't, don't do it, have mercy," I said
"Girl, I longed for this," he replied

In the next room, the mother-in-law
On the couch, my two children
On top of me, my father- in-law

I sought refuge with a different husband
Left the children behind

Widow Root grows in my neighborhood
The sorry of *widowhood* grows there too

Disgraceful mother, I was called
Shameless woman, I was called
Stone-hearted mother, I was called
I was denied custody of my children

Neither my children nor my faith forgave me

I could not tell anyone
My shame, my sorrow, my longing
At the age of thirty-eight
My heart refused to beat

The Cry from Limbo

I am the rebellious baby in Limbo

When they decided to burn my mother
I was in her womb
She struggled in her cell for three days
Her hand was on her belly
Her pain was my pain
Our emotions were one

We struggled for three days
She, for a reason
I, for no reason

They hauled my mother
To the stake to be tied
By the ropes of faith

She screamed nonstop:
    -I am pregnant
-I am with a child

Nobody heard
The people and
The Inquisition priest were deaf

The crowd screamed

"Burn"

"Burn"

The torch fell

Onto to the dry wood

My mother screamed

Suddenly

My world shuddered

I slipped out

With the water I was swimming in

Leaving the warmth of my mother

I dove into the flames

Manju Yadav

Manju Yadav is a multilingual poet and translator and writes poems & short stories in English, Hindi, and Spanish languages. Some of her Hindi & English poems and translations have been published in international poetry anthologies. She is a freelance translator from Spanish to Hindi and English, and vice-versa. Sheteaches Spanish as a second language in an International School in Hyderabad, India.

Love at the End

At the end what matters to a human

Is the sip of love to soothe his soul,

Drink with the cup of healing

To cement the scars of brokenness,

Sail through the valley of pain

To Travel the inner isle of peace,

At the end what happens to a human-

Is to sink deeper into his own heart,

stop taking the paths of El Dorado,

there is no charm of being true to self,

discover the treasure of your crossroads,

and find your beautiful inside and out,

At the end the human becomes own physician,

and looks around for more doses of love.

Oh! the love at the end brings the reinvention,

That is enough to make us whole again.

© Manju "Mann"

You Can't Mold Us In Your Shadow Anymore.

It's a million year old tale

When you started setting boundaries around us

Then you became self proclaimed master

And turned us in the dark shadows for years.

Now, when we are trying

We are growing

Becoming independent

Walking side by side to your shoulders

Denying everything you blamed we can't do

Defying every rules set by you

Now, we are athletic,

We are creative,

We are free-spirited

We are fierce and self-sufficient.

Exploring our shadows and plundering deeper to find our souls

To find more and more of self with every experience

You scare us with pictures of breaking families,

You ask us to recall motherly love for kids,

You urge to suppress our feelings for a fine conjugal balance,

You recount and reapply all your old weapons

To make us continue to be your shadows for million more years to come

Funny is that when you feel weaker

You start to blame on our character

And bring the religion between us

to fulfill self-centered desires

But time has exposed your old games of fuss and fouls.

And we have innovated ways to counter your scenarios.

We have learnt to show up self respect

And admit to resist for our growth

We have understood your trap to put us back in the old cage

And this time,

We have grown up firm and rigid than ever

Accepted to love and be committed to our future.

You can isolate us

Blame us,

Try to push us back, but

We will get up each time with a new fervor

We will raise voices more loud against every torture

We will not let you repeat history anymore.

No, you can't mold us in your shadow anymore.

Nalini Tandon

Dr. Nalini Tandon, is a medical doctor from India. After retirement from a successful and satisfying career, she is pursuing her other interests which include writing poetry. She is bilingual poet and writes both in English & Hindi.

Reflections of a Woman

That mirror hanging
On the wall so silently,
No frills, just facts
It says it all so valiantly

 The face that stares back at me
Seems strange.
The eyes are puffy,
Lashes not fluffy,
The shine has dimmed
Beneath the brow,
Still it's mine, I know.

The cheeks look deflated,
Few wrinkles surround
The mouth,
I observe with despair,
They seem so uncouth!

My bust not so round
A wee bit sagging,
The waist is broader
Its slimness, now lagging.

The veins on my hand
Like wrinkled roots they stand.
The skin is dry, looks parched,
And joints appear distorted.

 The nails are chapped,
My hair has lost its gloss.
It looks like a nest
Of white, grey, and black floss.

Toes are all de-shaped
With bunion and overlapping toe stumps,
Without separators
They cling and they clump.

The mirror tells me all,
But smiles quietly to say.
These are your landmarks of life,
You have passed your hurdles
With aplomb and style.

Homeless

Can you be homeless when you have a home?
The thought is ravaging my mind
Day and night, amidst others and alone
It's a thought so sublime

I started life with my love
We built a house and called it Home.
We filled it lovingly and with care
 With objects of our desire

We added cupboards, beds, and tables
All for us to be able
To live with harmony and peace
With togetherness and ease.

There was the pitter-patter of our girls
Things strewn around everywhere
Their sweet faces and curls
Brought smiles, despite the constant care.

But time had wings, it flew away
The girls are gone, their rooms empty and desolate
We clutched the memories
They melted in our hearts, mocking our fate

Desire to be with the family
Be together again
Dominated our thoughts eerily
Wringing our hearts with pain

We packed our bags, we flew to distant lands
To meet our children!
Spending life with them,
But distancing from our brethren.

Now we live out of suitcases
Roaming hither and thither,
Seemingly we have won many life's races
But did we? My mind tarries and wonders here

When I return to the home we made
I see the desolate books, lying quietly
Once they were read and re-read,
Hoping to be picked up again they now just wait
patiently

Each corner, each table, each sofa, each chair
Seems shrouded in sorrow missing our loving care.
That bindi in the drawer once adorned my forehead,
I saw it dust covered lying forlornly on the bed

I walk past the kitchen cabinet,
Tarry a little and touch caressingly
My old tea kettle, and the dinner set
Still smelling the hot ginger tea, and the snacks spread
lavishly

Bed sheets, blankets, and the pillow
Are lying covered and still,
The colors have faded to brown and yellow
Their musty smell, filling my nostril.

Each nook, each corner seems to ask
Where are the joy and the laughter?
Why do you tarry o' mistress?
Come dance; fill us with fragrance that we desire.

I open my suitcase, now my constant companion
With memories and sorrow, but no fuss
And wonder once again
I have this home, so why am I homeless?

Kimberly Crafton

Kimberly Crafton is a writer of narrative essays, letters, articles, and cultural guide books. She is a respected leader in cultural projects - always focused on connecting people to their own forgotten histories, to their ancestors, their neighbors, their communities, their world.

Life is a Folding

Like of dough

    fold in half

    push, turn

    again in half

    push, turn

Like of hands

    sitting quiet on the lap

    clasped tight

    as if in prayer

Life is a folding

    of letters written

    to the dear

    to the hungered after

    to the injured by

Life is a folding

    like of bills in the pocket

carelessly or with greatest care

like of clothes

neatly packed to go

or hastily thrown in home's drawer

This folding

of time -

trying to make it fit into our comprehension

of dreams -

tucking them away for a better time

of presence -

making ourselves smaller so as not to offend

This folding keeps us busy

so busy

for we can never be still

lest something of us

take up more room than it should

Life is a folding

    like of table cloths

    and linens and handmade doilies

    everything we make to cover what is there

    in order to make it more beautiful

    like of window shutters

    closet doors and room dividers

    everything we pull tight

    in order to keep the eyes of the word

    from seeing too far inside

Standing at the Desk

I'm standing at the desk

Standing politely near the desk

Not at the desk - that would be too threatening

I'm standing imploringly between

Her room door and the nurses desk

That calm look on my face

Practiced in vain hope of ever perfecting it

Who me? Oh yes - yes, we DO need something

(Urgently!)

...if it's not too much trouble to call the doctor

(Dear God please help us!)

...yes, I know you are so busy and trying so hard

...yes, please... as soon as you have a second..."

Now I'm standing <u>at</u> the desk

Desperate to speak to someone

Sculpting my facial muscles

To hide all the fear my disbelief

her life is slipping away

Opening my eyes brightly

To disguise the anger

The helplessness raging inside me

the world moves blindly on

I stand smooth like a marble statue
Unassuming at the desk
The only place we are given to bring
Our supplications

>*won't somebody please help her*

You finally arrive
Wearing a face sculpted to look like it cares
Wearing a mask that says it wants to help
but alas cannot
I watch your cold blooded lips form words like
Policies and Procedures
and Patience
Lethal words spoken through a forked tongue
Death-sentence words spoken as if they could soothe

My castaway soul begins to scream
I am screaming your name, Jonah

>*Jonah... Jonah*

For I know my sister and I caught
Caught in the belly of this corporate killer whale
Digestive juices begin to rise up our legs
Just a few more hours and she will be gone
And I will be the throaty broken cry a seagull
Dancing dangerously low across the dark hungry water.

Erina Çoku

Erina Çoku has finished the high school "Pjetër Budi" in Burrel
(1994-1998) and studied for Language and Literature
(Linguistic profile) at the Faculty of History and Philology, in
Tirana University (1999-2003).

She has published two poetry books: "Krahës'kanëëngjëjt e
mi" (My angels are without wings" ("Toena", 1997) and
"Gjurma e gjethes" (The leaf's trace) ("Botimet WestPrint",
2011).

Her poems and reviews are published in different literary
magazines, literary anthologies and other literary mediums:
"Poeteka", "Milosao", "Radi and Radii", "Poets and Writers",
"Botimet Shqiptare", "Fjala Review", "Emathia", "Kultplus",
"Tetova news", "Darsiani.com", "Mapo", "Telegraf", "Dita",
"Observer.com", "Albmendimiarts.com", "Shekulli", "Tirana
Post", "Shkodra Press", "Zemra Shqiptare", "Gentlewomen",
"Fjalashqipe.com", "Koha", "Adunis Poetry", "Revista
Letrare", "ArsAlbanica"ecc.

She was part of different poetic activities: "Poeteka",
"Portikuletrar", "Festivaliipoezisësëpabotueme",
"Verëdhepoezi", TransformArt",
"TakimetNdërkombëtareAzemShkreli", "Këngëdhepoezi",
"Ditët e Naimit" ecc.

She had an artistic collaboration (as editor and as creative writer) for the descriptive texts of the Italian artist Luca Morici paintings presented in the exhibition "Il dolore" (The Pain), 2012.

She is editor of many poetry books. For many years worked as editor at publishing house "Pegi. Currently works at Diaspora Publishing Center.

The Longing

The longing for you is here,
I feed it
with the breathe that doesn't arrive
your warm skin
I hold it
with the looks that don't enter
your faraway pores.

The longing for you is here,
a young animal,
(what should I do with it?)
sees with big eyes
doesn't know to kiss
doesn't know to hug
doesn't know even to silence.

The longing for you is here,
a wild bird
(if I let it free)
it will find you
eat your flesh
corrode your bones
your hot blood will glut it.

The longing for you is here,

is being created,

(tomorrow, I don't know what will be),

It takes my body, my mind, my breath.

It's here.

Come.

Come take it.

Confessional

Hope to see you soon, he said.
Must be a land on the moon, I said.

He stared at me – to him I stared.
We both were lost – to loss was praised.

He walked away – his eyes remained.
I walked away carrying his gaze.

His eyes are here – his body so far.
He must be missing that eye to eye.

He left – I left. His eyes were theft.
I am a sinner – I must confess.

And like a confessor I must reveal.
I plead guilty for having stolen.

Have I the right for more or less?
I need his body to confess.

© Erina Çoku

Alka Prakash

Alka Prakash is a poet and critic of literature. She is a lecturer in Dr. Rajendra Singh Rajju Bhaiya State University, Prayagraj, India. She has published many books especially on women issues.

Waiting is like the Text of a Letter

(Translated into English from Hindi by Shamenaz)

Waiting

Is not

a mere word.

At every moment

at every day

months and years

we are living

in this hope

a little bit of disperse.

After being disperse

It is raging

like a fire

and our dreams

are ripens in it.

Waiting

Is like text of a letter

In which there's written

many unwritten

which makes us

a bit breezy.

Oh!

If there's would have been no waiting

then this life

would have been

so monotonous

so meaningless.

If there's would have been no waiting

then everyday

this physique would have

changed it's form

it wouldn't have been

so white

this sheet of mind.

In rain

we would think

about out that solitary times

in which

we have been drenched

and became

more impatient.

In this ruthless hour

It has been long await

now

please come.

Oh! Cyber

(Translated into English from Hindi by Shamenaz)

Rivers will refuse to fall in the Oceans

they are upset

Flower will refuse to bloom

they are angry

When you don't see the crime then

this is the only way left.

The cloud will refuse to rain,

and the trees will not bear fruits,

and before kids refuse to laugh

don't snatch their childhood Oh! ICT.

Tell me how to stop your misuse?

do you know it's horror

Children when learning modem, CPU, floppy, hard disk

when suddenly see porn

become distracted.

You have increased the responsibilities of parents

you have bestowed

a serious responsibility

which they will carry with ease.

Iva Santini

Iva Santini likes to dive deeep into the spaces within many dimensions inside her body. She travels to those landscapes and then transfers those images and energies into material words.

Impermeable Fragility

(Manifesto of a wild orchid)

Sounds lived beneath her skin.

Special types of sounds.

Every sound has a shape,

and its sounds were prickly.

They hurt her skin.

That's when they say

they wouldn't be in her shoes.

In the bathroom,

when you lie motionless long enough

on these light brown tiles,

they become blue, dark blue, very dark blue

 and soon you no longer feel them,

but you start to sink.

And while many would be intimidated by this

overwhelming event, she loves to dive.

She loves to dive.

She loves diving so much that the very dark blue has

crept under her skin and melted her thorns.

This dark blue bites and breaks bones,

 penetrates the central features of the body

and conquers the fragile heart.

When she came to the surface

somewhere near the shipyard

and touched the bottom,

dragging the sea with her,

the sea would burst,

and leaves would sprout from her skin,

 the only way she could step on the earthen grass.

Why doesn't that fragility disintegrate

 together with all those unheard cries

of skin that rests over the prickly sounds.

Why didn't she crumble herself

and sprinkle herself on the surface of her balm

 and kiss him forever.

Why branches always grow out of it,

 why the leaves adorn it and

why it doesn't fall anymore.

Because she loved that land

and all her bare feet

squeezing her cheeks, sandy,

wet grassy, muddy, and spiky.

And why she talked.

Why she has to express herself.

Why she sings to the rhythm of her prickly skin sounds.

Why she massages and anoints them.

Somewhere in the depths there is relaxation.

Relaxation so strong that it can carry
 the most beautiful sounds.
Sounds that the body is not home to,
 but love to travel with.
Sounds that a woman does not hear,
because they are her.
Deer and airspace hear it and the sun hears it.
Only wild orchids stay true to their lionesses,
mares and anacondas.
Only wild orchids,
after miles of mountains and valleys,
walk the white shaggy carpet
of bare feet in a dried mud dress
 and sip the rarest Chinese teas
 on soft pillows in the company
of never-before-seen animals
 in the wilderness of a first-visited jungle.
Her fingers melt the skin
and leave deep marks on the soul.
They penetrate to the heart
 and as the iron turns to honey,
she takes out the colorful spices
 she sprinkles it on, dips her index finger
 into the sandwich of her palate

and the middle of her tongue,

and becomes the taster

of another newly baked heart.

Unlocked Dream

(Song that expresses how I experience art of Brazilian Jiu Jitzu)

In the middle of your dream, you stood in front of the mirrors

mirrors

The ground did not move

The mirror pulled you

You built walls

You were looking for ways out

You watched your reflection

But you were alone

You didn't swim for the air

There is no exit on the surface

You knew you were a dream

And the key looked at you from the bottom

In the middle of your dream

You dived all the way to the bottom

The ground did not move

But it dissolved

In the middle of your awakening

You kept the reflection alone

And you saw it then

Another unlocked dream

Neerja Sachdev

Dr. Neerja Sachdev is an Associate Professor, Head of the Department in English, S. S. Khanna Girls' Degree College, Prayagraj. She has been teaching since 1980 and has more than 40 years of experience. She has a passion for writing poems and writes both in English as well as Hindi. She has published many poems and has participated in many international Poetry festivals. She has attended many Seminars/Conferences in India and abroad. She has also published many research papers in reputed journals.

Hope

Hope is a ship that steers your life.

It kindles the spark that gives you foresight,

To outline your future with full might,

Without tribulations affecting your hindsight.

Crying over spilt milk is reminiscing,

Sweet are the uses of adversity is strengthening,

Every cloud has a silver lining is infusing

A dawn in life, with hopes invigorating.

These mottos are attached as aphorism

In mankind, always standing apart with a dictum,

With precepts, proverbs and life's maxims,

Trying to translate hopes with an apothegm.

Hope resides in each soul.

And tweets and twitters with a goal.

It stands through torrid storms,

And lingers long, keeping your spirit warm.

No matter what destiny has in store for you,

You have to stand upright and foresee

A hope that lies buried underneath

Reminding, 'Survival of the fittest' stands right beneath.

Summer is vibrant with the arrival of monsoon,

Monsoons shower the hopes of new growth.

Winter lies dormant but never loses hope

Echoing, 'if winter comes can spring be far behind'!

Hope gives you wings to fly,

To float with dream soaring high.

Hopes are soothing winds that whispers nigh

Singing melodiously, be optimistic, and never cry.

Yesterdays are past, tomorrow never comes

Today is the present, make it a legend.

Never dread the past, have no fears of future.

For Hope is the faith, that never abandons you dear.

Hope is the recipe for success,

Be strong in trouble, accept challenges, and never bend,

Put up your safety belts to meet bumpy roads ahead,

For hope is the last thing ever lost or dead.

Fear

Where the mind is without fear?

Can you hear it with your ear?

The journey of life traverses

With upheavals here and there.

Life is shrouded in a bundle of mysteries.

A mother welcomes the birth of her child.

But fears the baby steps taken by might.

Being possessive and apprehensive with fright.

Life is fraught with tribulations.

Will we overcome them with adulations?

Will the parts of the body function in merriment?

And not decay in life's detriment?

Going to school is a pleasure.

Appearing for examinations is a terror.

Climbing each rung of the ladder

 Is Fraught with errors?

Having courage to take a venture,

Makes you run through the adventure.

Erupting goose pimples, qualms and jitters

Will I accomplish it, fills me with fritters.

Degrees, Gold medals, Trophies lead to disquietude.

'Cause they apprehend the threat of solicitude.

Achieving them forebodes incertitude,
Striving to possess those needs effort with quietude.

Marriages are made in Heaven.
But they are earthly bonds with vows seven.
They steer the ship of life without consternation,
But the vicissitudes in life are never without
perturbation.

Love, faith, compassion and courageousness,
Culminates the conjugal life with dauntlessness.
Children bridge this gap with boldness
By their fearlessness, gallantry, impudence and
doughtiness.
Wealth, Health, Prosperity and Happiness.
Are they all the companions of the soul?
Is the soul, a spirit in search of hope?
Seeking Peace, Eternal Peace without scope.

Basking in a toll free life with daily bread
Torments the memory, the warder of the brain with
dread.
Apprehensions, conflicts and tensions are the tools
That turns the milk sour for fools.

The journey of life will get over, why fear death?
It will steal your heart and leave you bereft.

The soul, lying buried will leave your life in a moment.

Unscathed, unheard upward to Hell or Heaven.

Purwanti Kusumaningtyas

Purwanti Kusumaningtyas lives in Salatiga, Central Java, Indonesia. She writes poems and short stories in Bahasa Indonesia and English.

Closure

The rise in the East initiates the joyful adventure.
The roosters' proud cries, the birds' gay chirps, songs, and whistles,
The greeting breeze, the waves of the leaves,
The dancing butterflies, the crawling lizards,
Send the bats and the night birds back to their beds.
As the waking half of the world stirs and moves,
The other half takes their rest for the next day's acts.

The two halves are the routes.
I crawl, walk, run, jump, dance,
and even fall and rise and fall and rise again
in between them.
I got wounded and get healed
And was hurt and recovered
And again and again and again.

The ripe tangerine in the West
Tells a lot about the whole journey.

All kinds of deeds and mistakes

I have done all the way

No need to be sad or full of regrets

As whatever paths were offered on the day

Are useful for the strength of my lungs, heart, and legs.

The simple chirps of the night birds star the darkness,

the soft claps of the bats' wings lull the tired ones.

Time has come to rest and be calm.

The bed is waiting; my eyes are drooping.

I walk slowly, yet triumphantly

I lay down and sigh,

Whispering good night to close the day.

Anna Maria Dall'Olio

MA Languages: English and Portuguese (Pisa, 1985), BA Letters (Pisa, 2004. Summer scholarship in Portuguese Language and Culture (Facultade de Letras, Lisboa, 1982). She has been teaching English in Italian high schools since 1987.

She has devoted herself to fiction, poetry and playwriting. In 2005 she was ranked second in "Hanojo - via Rendevuo", a Vietnamese cultural competition for the millennial celebration of Hanoj (1010-2010). In addition, she was ranked first/second/third in lots of literary competitions for her Italian poems (2006-2019).

She published a collection of short stories, "In vettura! ("All aboard!", 2021) and a novel, "Segreti" ("Secrets", 2018). Moreover, she published 5 collections of poems:"Sì shabby chic" ("So shabby chic", 2018), "L'acqua Opprime" ("Water oppresses", 2016), "Fruttorto Sperimentale" ("Experimental Food Forest", 2016), "Latte & Limoni" ("Milk & Lemons", 2014), "L'angoscia del pane" ("Bread is anguish", 2010). Finally, she wrote 2 plays, "Evoluzioni" ("Evolutions", 2019) and "Tabelo" ("Table", 2006), both dealing with mobbing as a supreme artistic form.

Up to now she has written in Italian, Esperanto and English (even if she hasn't published in this language yet). Some of her poems mix Italian with Tuscan dialects, Furlan and even Latin.

Dall'Olio's dramatic and poetic interests are focussed on reality as well as society, even if she deals with her own life. As far as poetry is concerned, the poet's literary tradition needs to be kept in mind before writing: it is always the topic to point out the most convenient poetic style of each poem: yet, topics are up-to-date, and so final layouts are bound to be unexpected. As for fiction, Dall'Olio deals with reality as much as fantasy, mixing different genres of prose and poetry.

Several Italian poets and literary critics have expressed their favorable opinions on her works. She published her poems in sundry anthologies and for a few literary magazines as well as webzines.

Italian scholar Gianfranco Cotronei published "Le sirene di cartone di Anna Maria Dall'Olio" ("Anna Maria Dall'Olio's cardboard sirens", 2017), a monograph about her literary career.

Web site: www.annamariadallolio.it

Gezi Park, Milk and Lemons

Tree-lined square,
a shopping centre will bloom instead:
the riot breaks out.

For crowds & crowds
milk & lemons will bloom
out of the windows.

Out of the web do drip
legs apart dancing
plastic postures.

In rival scarfs
ant capitalists
& veiled women.

Hand in hand
kemalists & Curds
circle dance.

Everybody nobody
gazes on the flag:
in the square, trees.

Angry angels

So sudden statues:
Turkish magic.

How much semi hope
In harsh dictatorship.

On the Razor's Edge, Iceland

Something sighed
a flowing river is falling
foam flows out.

Too high is the national debt
too high are interest rates
too low are median incomes.

The toxic torture in the deepest depths.
either lava or corn fields.
On the razor's edge, blades of grass

Helen Sarita

Helen Sarita is a Filipino writer who has a deep passion for Poetry at her mature stage. She is a mother of five well-raised children and a grandmother of six. Sarita had already published two poetry books in Lulu entitled "It's About Time" and "Language of Love.". She is also in several Anthology books published in the USA and India. She was once a contributor in the poetry section in the Filipino Expats Magazine and Kabayan Weekly Newspaper in Dubai, UAE. Some of her poems were translated into French, Turkish, Spanish, Greek, and Manipuri- a native Dialect in India.

She is the first Filipino Woman who virtually gathers Filipino Poets to be united as one and connect them to other poetry groups internationally. She encourages other poets by awakening their love in poetry by exposing them to the domain of the poetry world arena. As for her, literature must not vanish but has to be nurtured and preserved. She called the group she created "Filipino Poets in Blossoms," which she named after Blossoms Journal International Magazine, to which she is the Founder and the CEO.

Be Proud I Am Your Friend

Sincere every now and then
Especially to a true friend
I am not lavish with my compliments.
Everyone deserves an honest comment.

I appreciate you when you are right
Do not hesitate to correct yourself
when you are wrong
for the welfare of a real friend
no matter if you get offended.

If I have something to adore about you
If your blessings from above just flow
I do not claim God's gift is not equally shared.
He just wanted to test if I am sincere.

I am glad of the wonderful things you have
I feel bad when some fight your back.
Ready to give my sweet caress,
Especially in times of your sadness.

My ultimate care makes you feel better.
My advice is an important matter.

Being honest and being sincere

Makes you proud that I am your friend.

When My Spirit Commands

I write when I like my words to care

Like a consoling hand on your shoulder

When I get tense about the days ahead

And I want my soul and mind to escape.

When I have a roller coaster emotion

That suddenly goes up, suddenly goes down.

I write not just on my peaceful bed.

But even when I'm on board in a noisy ship.

I write when I want to shout to the whole world.

And spread my words across the globe.

I write to express my immense gratification,

And share my creations with all nations.

I write when I like to convey gratitude to my friends.

Who look up not only to my weaknesses but my

worthiness?

Not only when the sky studded with stars and moon

I write even my dark night is blue and is in the gloom.

And amid my busy min and lazy hands.

I write when my spirit commands.

Manisha Singh

Dr Manisha Singh is a bilingual poet, who writes both in English and Hindi. She is currently teaching English in NKVI College in Lucknow, Uttar Pradesh with a teaching experience of 20 years. She has obtained her PhD degree and has also qualified NET. She has published several research articles and poems in National & International journals and has presented scholarly papers in National and International Conferences. Her area of specialization is Indian Literature. She is the Vice President of "The Progressive, Literary & Cultural Society", an International forum, promoting Global Literature & Culture. Recently she has edited the Multilingual poetry Anthology.

Contemplation

Ohm- in itself a Supreme Being-

A whole universe

It's discourse, definition

And Perfection

Has ever contemplated

To sigh at the Sight

Of its extreme Expectation

With all its Perfection.

Oh no! Never at all.

As it's quintessentialism is

Implicit and rationale

But the neo-paradigms

Of abduction, lust and

Animosity is:

Fulfledging it's architectural

wings- engulfing

the whole lot of

So called- Supreme animal.

Oh! this term has become

Too… stale

And only it's Fossils are

Preserved as

Specimens in laboratories

Museums and Classics.

What a Beautiful World

Why do we only dream of a beautiful world?

He should create and do what's worth.

All contemplate but none is assiduous,

To make this world a blissful land.

All of us need to now realize, mere mediocrity won't

now suffice.

Blessings have always been disguised,

Endowed by the essence of excellence and

Ambitiousness to bring peace in the world,

Understanding to be an uber-human being.

Trustworthiness and truthfulness are the

Ideals which make us an immortal being.

Faithfulness leads to forgiveness,

Unique person we all can be.

Love and loyalty too will lead to,

Warm-hearted and compassionate being

Obliging whomever we come across

Radiant and radical for a rosy cause

Liberal and lion heartedness makes one

Dauntless and courageous to serve human.

Glória Sofia

Glória Sofia, is a dreamer as most poets. Born in the city of Praia in Cape Verde, South Africa.She graduated in Engineering and Environmental Management in the Azores. She has been writing since childhood. Among other poetry sites she collaborates with the online newspaper of magazines in the world. She was nominated to apply for RMAPAI.

She has been invited to 3 University from Boston (April 2019). Harvard University, Tufts University and Boston University for reading and conversation about genre and literature.

She also represented her country Cape Verde in VIII Conference in Portuguese Language Literature UMass Boston, gala cidad la paz Bolivia 2020.

Her poetry has been translated into more than 15 languages, in 2020 she win one prize for Union Mundial Poetas Paz Liberdade She participated in International Poetry Festival in (Curtea de Arges) Romania (2016), (Istanbul) Turkey (2017), Ditet &

Naimit Macedonia / Albania (2018), festival internacional Bangladesh.

Her Books include:

1. Lacos de Poesias, Editora Brial, Rotterdam, Holanda, 2015

2. Abriel, Editora Brial, Rotterdam, Holanda, 2018

3. Urso Haby, United P.C, Rotterdam, Holanda, 2019

4. Mar de Cabo Verde, Vakxikon Publications, Atenas, Greece, 2021

Independence

Freedom is usually celebrated

In this month of warmth and remembrance

It is customary to hear the lashed voices

Caught in the waves of angry breezes

The cry is usually sung

And with the whip anthem

The mountains of poverty

With the arms of poetry

Scream every humanity

That withers the flowers of the islands

Brave arms are usually applauded

That let the flag dance in the sky

The emergence of being free chewed

Fear intoxicated by tears.

Sweats swelled the icy hope

It is often said that in the end

At the end

The heart sprouts the smile of a free country

In the Lap of Volcanoes

Discouraged find

The color of courage

That transposes the revolt

Iron and harmonica rebelled

Against authority

Established

Too human to understand
Thorn in the feet
Ripped hunger eyes

Today July 5, 1975

Usually celebrates

The independence of a country

That the wind rests

The secret of the free islands

In the glow of the sea

Eternal night with Covid 19

Sky is no longer a volcano that expels the sun

Souls echoed through the nose with dead green

En not green for hope

The mountains hid the clouds

Moon gave birth to the melody of light

The sea excruciates the colors

Memories flutter with voracious waves

The stars burn my feel

I know I will never dawn

The moonlit night perpetuated me with corona

What if poetry and peace

And if the galaxies exploded

In the chest of memory

And if the memories spread on the wall of being

And if they got together again

Just stay there again

Hot and painful memories

I simply begged some kind of sound

To shake the heart of memory

The silent memories that blind me

When the wind tells the sea

That the years ago the dreams

And that poetry resides in prison

And not in freedom

That poetry lives in hate and not i peace

I want only sad wind to scream that: De poetry is frees

Amelia Cayul Tranamil

Amelia Cayul Tranamil is a poet from Chile – Mapuche Nation. She is a bilingual poet and writes in Spanish and native language of Mapuche nation, Mapudungun. She is an indigenous activitist and the Ambassador of Identity of Mapuche Culture. She is a global representative of Mapuche culture. She is also an ancestral/Indigenous Mapuche Kitchen chef. She is a PLCS Latin American Representative.

Land People

From the depths that it harbors

The earth, a race of people, is liberated.

The blood watching the rays of the sun

A different blood that pumps your heart

They walked very dark trails

Where there was a light that guides his path causing his
destiny to change
Turning their blood to wine

Where will we find the exit?

If we don't find it, our life is lost!

The cold runs through our naked torso,

How will our race accept the world

It's hard to accept reality

As our people are mercilessly disappearing

Our environment every day looks like hell and wekufu

 they are already serving you

Liberation to our spirit!

Liberation to our body!

Liberation to our land!

Liberation because today something begins!

Idiom

Speak my language

Mapudugun, my voice and

My body

Shouts!! Between

Cerro, huge hill

Where are the trees

Native people!!

It pierces and it sounds

Between the mountains

My spirit, breathe the scent

Of each Ancestral tree

Pewen

Mapue

Boldo

Canelo

"The knowledge is here"

My ancestors are sad

Children and youth

That they know our language

Mapugen ka Mapugetan

Hristina Cvetanoska

Hristina Cvetanoska graduated Acting at the Faculty of Dramatic Arts in Skopje, as well as Italian language and Literature at the Faculty of Philology in Skopje. She got her MA (2019) in Theatre Studies at the Faculty of Dramatic Arts – Skopje. For three years she was working as an Assistant Professor at this same faculty. Now she works as a Macedonian Language and Culture teacher in NOVA International Schools in Skopje, Macedonia.

Do You Know How Distances Are Embraced?

Do you know how distances are embraced?

first, you erase the borders.

All of them, spatial and time,

geographic and non-geographic,

those of the mind and those of the heart,

and those you do not want to hear about.

Then, you try to shape the void,

You measure - a few meters of peace,

And a few more wistfulness.

Your hands are drawing in the emptiness

and if you have at least a bit of fantasy as I do,

(if you are lucky not to be betrayed by inaccurate
memories)

you will embrace my distance

as you embrace the closest to your heart.

For its everything that remained to us

after countless attempts for closeness,

distance became our closest one.

You ask me,

why I embrace emptiness?

I tell you,

I do not know what oblivion is like.

I do not know what forgetting is like.

I just know what distances are like

and the emptiness between them,

and the particles of air

In which I kiss you,

and the kilometers outrun by every thought

just to reach you.

I told you. And I will tell you again -

I do not know how to embrace oblivion,

I do not know how to grip something

that does not exist.

You do exist, so tell me

how to turn you into emptiness.

when I have you with all your wholeness.

In my loneliness

you do exist, though

I do not know how. There is no way how.

If you ask me again as in the night

before I left,

what I write about most often,

I will not tell you

About wistfulness

About emptiness

About loss.

These verses know

How many distances they brought together

And I will tell you

About arrivals.

About closeness

About togetherness.

Dalila Hiaoui

Dalila Hiaoui, Morocco Italian poet writer. Poet and writer, teacher of Arabic language and culture. She works at a United Nations agency in Rome.

She has been organizing and leading since 2002 the bilingual literary salon J'nan Argana (Argan's Paradise), and she is General Secretary and assistant for the Arab world at the World Poetry Movement.

She collaborates with several Arab magazines and newspapers as a columnist and writer.

She has published 43 books as an author and co-author and a three-volume Arabic textbook with UniNettuno International University. Her poems have been translated in 13 languages.

Lavender

When has the light of the lighthouse ever begged for
attention,
From the heap of ruins?
Or to be, sometimes or forever, covered
By the broken wing?
You aren't a throne,
You aren't a crown…
And not even on the face of a medal!
You aren't the elixir of life….
And not even a smile that can remain on one's lips
Forever either.
Unfold your sails and get away from the shore,
From which you thought of its purity
As if it was leprosy.
Your absence
Will not make the towers of the fortress a ruin.
The brambles will not thrive in paradise……
In the place of lavender.
Your absence will only increase
The museums of impairments,
Adding more idols to the shelves!

Debra Mascarenhas

Debra Mascarenhas is basically from India but residing in United Arab Emirates since many years. She has published two poetry collections entitled as *Whispers from the Heart* and *Sail into the World of My Poems*. She is a regular participant on various poetry sites and magazines. She is a PLCS UAE Representative.

Miss You

How do I say of much I miss him?

Miss, you is nothing compared to the void left in my life

Eleven years have gone by

and never a day,

never a moment when I don't miss you.

I do try and pretend you will come back,

I do pretend you are on a holiday without me,

I do pretend you are working in a country where I cannot

reach you,

For I miss you very much.

The eyes have run dry,

No more tears I can cry,

I accept that one day we will meet

Until that day I miss you.--

Mystery of Missing Girl

It was a dark and stormy night
the street lights flickering,
the branches on the trees swaying
as the leaves fell to the ground
due to the strong wind,
while the rains lashed,
the streets, flooding the lanes
bringing all traffic to a standstill.

The electricity went off as the pole fell down
the whole town is dark,
little candle lights burning
shadows moving behind the curtains.

Crisis management is on the roads
with the aid of the police
fixing the fallen electricity pole,
with the rains lashing
their work is hampered.

A loud crash heard down the street
the police look towards the sound,
they can see nothing
no movement, no more sound
there is no improvement with stormy weather,

it is lightning and thundering non-stop.

A chopper flies past them
and then a siren is heard far in the distance
lights flickering the ambulance is speeding
goes down the street,
a tree has crashed on a house
and an old lady is injured.

The street drains are overflowing
carrying with it all the dirt from the gutter,
along with it came a huge bag
that got stuck near the police car,
the streets lights come on
and the police find a body
that was missing for a week.

The mystery of the missing girl
is now discovered in a garbage bag.

Zaneta Varnado Johns

Zaneta Varnado Johns (aka Zan) a 2-time bestselling author who believes that every word shared is an opportunity to love. Her debut book of poetry, Poetic Forecast: Reflections on Life's Promises, Storms, and Triumphs (WSA Publishing, 2020) became a Hot New Release on Amazon and topped Amazon's Bestseller List at #1 in six category. Johns is a co-author in the #1 International Bestsellers, Voices of the 21st Century: Resilient Women Who Rise and Make a Difference (WSA Publishing, 2021). She is also a contributing author in Jane Austen: an anthology of thoughts & opinions (Purple Stone Press, 2021). Her poems appear in Fine Lines Literary Journal and Open Door Magazine, among numerous others. Recognized by the University of Colorado as one of its 2007 Women Who Make a Difference, Johns is a retired human resources leader. Stay tuned for Zan Johns' highly anticipated second book of poetry, After the Rainbow: Golden Poems (Prolific Pulse Press LLC) and her appearance in Voices of the 21st Century: Conscious Caring Women Who Make a Difference (WSA Publishing), publication February 22, 2022. Johns resides in Westminster, Colorado, USA. Website: www.zanexpressions.com

Not Her Fault

She left for the party looking like a million bucks

She returned home like a discarded penny—

her appearance was amuck.

Her elation swelled when they first drove away.

She had lustful hopes after a long stressful day.

They laughed, they danced, they ate and drank.

When a handsome man winked at her,

to him and his ego, it felt like a prank.

Her once cheerful companion did a one-eighty turn.

His demeanor was all anger—a fiery rage that could
burn.

He grabbed his beautiful queen and reduced her to fear.

Like a ragdoll, she went limp as her eyes filled with
tears.

He said things to her not worthy of repeat.

His words were as harsh as a drumlin's rapid beat.

Her lovely dress was torn, her arm needed a sling.

Every time she wiped her eyes,

the fresh abrasions would sting.

She wondered what she'd done to cause such a scene.

She assumed it was her fault,

though like grass in summer, his envy was green.

She softly said, "I'm sorry," holding onto her purse.

He furiously snatched her by the arm,

making the painful strain worse.

Her strand of pearls was now broken,

but not as much as her heart.

She'd ignored all the signs

that he revealed from the start.

They drove home in silence—

he never spoke a word.

She thought about their last dance

and the awful things she'd heard.

She slowly stumbled inside, ran a bath, and got some ice.

He brewed a cup of tea to sweetly serve her,

pretending to be nice.

She sat in utter silene—her lips could not move.

There was nothing he could do,

and her deep pains…he could not soothe.

She knew it was time to leave her toxic man.

She fervently prayed throughout the night,

She woke up determined and said, "I CAN!"

No Footprints

When life's squabbles fiercely erupt

When your burdens become unbearable

When your pain is too intense

When no words provide comfort

When the despair is overwhelming

When your light becomes dim

When your sunken eyes are swollen

When dark nights lead to darker days

When looking down feels better than up

When you are gently lifted and carried

When your way comes out of no way

When you can't recall progression

When troubled water no longer troubles you

When your season of trials ends

When your tears dry up

When you look down, perplexed

When you see footprints that are not yours

There is no need to look again

You know the answer—

You left no footprints because God carried you through.

Bridie Breen

Bridie Breen is Athlone, Irish born and Manchester UK matured writer. Her background is the field Mental Health Nursing. She enjoys poetry in all its forms, poetic prose, haiku, short scripts, co-poetry and monologues. Media platforms Soundcloud, Facebook, also http//: www.celticthoughts.co.uk   She regular participants of online poetry forums and open mic sessions. She is a member of Manchester Irish Writers. She has published poems in many anthologies and interested in human condition, migrant voices, justice, valuing our planet.

Timeout

A woman grown invisible

questions the very essence of her existence

Peruses time now spent or lent to others

Years uncoil umbilical. Twines afresh in monotone

Being is all there is. Body battered as fuselage in battle

She wonders if profligacy has come back to haunt

Constant giving, never-ending availability

Now comes merging days of emptying

where own soul scrapes a barrel bottom

Resilience soaks away. Life scourged to bone

Eyes too tired to weep

All to be said, can be done in one breath

She sighs as flesh enwraps

an ageing frame no longer familiar.

Wonder of life

Wonder of life fills every space in mind

It's only right that hope goes hand in hand

with love, to outlast all other emotions

That courage comes from

an inner reserve, to surprise, uplift

and strengthen when least expected.

It's only right that love remains constant

as stars that fill the night sky

And, hope is a beacon that lights up our path.

Brings us to our destination,

sometimes gently, sometimes firm, always truthful.

It's only right that those things beyond

our comprehension, are left awash with

wonder, of a kind that fills every space in mind

© Bridie

Jill Sharon Kimmelman

Jill Sharon Kimmelman is a two-time Pushcart Prize nominee in Poetry, (2017 & 2021). She has been nominated for Best Of The Net 2018. Her publication credits include, Vita Brevis Press, Spillwords Press, Fine Lines, Better Than Starbucks Magazine, Love Of Food Magazine, Poetic Musings, Yasou! A Celebration Of Life, The Poet Magazine, ILA Magazine, The New York Parrot, Prolific Pulse Press, Delaware Boots On The Ground, Greenville Hockessin Life Magazine, Heart Beat, & "A Safe Brave Space, Garden of Nero, Writing In A Woman's Voice. Beginning in 2020, Jill has contributed back cover text to several individual poetry books & an ever-growing collection of anthologies. Several of her poems have been the framework for her playlist of poetry videos, created by Sparrow Productions, Sri Lanka. All of her poetry videos are archived on Youtube

Her culinary arts background is evident throughout her poetry & in conversations. She lives in Delaware, USA with her husband Tim, & is a proud mother of her son Jordan.

A Woman's Prayer

God, please

Do not let me live so long that everything I love is taken

from me

piece by piece

take me with you before I ever stand

staring into the abyss of my own child's grave

when exhausted by the deaths of lifelong friends

I tire of going to their funerals—simply stop

when technology becomes a labyrinth—I find myself

lost within

when aged, alone, unglued and unfocused

the vitality of my mind defies my ancient body

leaving me a shell of the girl in the mirror

Let my eyes still see rainbows and sly grins

on the angelic face of our precious grandson

allow me the gift of one more magnificent sunrise and

sunset

before you take the last of my waning vision

grant me time to witness the end of an era

where random-hate crimes and "mass shootings"

have become our "new-normal"

Please bless me with strength as I hold my husbands's
hand
when the last word he softly speaks is my name—then
no more

Lord please
deliver a peace that will drift over me
calm me
hush the whispers of my unspoken fears
allow me to close my eyes in trust that the morning will
deliver
a brilliant beautiful peace-filled day.

©Jill Sharon Kimmelman
Spring 2021

Missing Your Poet's Voice

(For Munmun Samanta, my dearest sister Sam.)

You are cherished.
May we forever embrace & celebrate
 the contents of each other's hearts.
Friend to friend, sister to sister,
 poet to poet…forever linked
Bring back the stories—
those slice-of life poems
from the heart of your village
Portraits of yesterdays
that fill me with joy always
deliver smiles—send me
into paroxysms of delicious belly laughter.
Those tales of large cars
painted in pinks, peach, melons,
waltz blue ladies departing beauty shops
proudly bearing stiff bouffant hair
children in rumpled uniforms
feet and hair flying on Mercury's wings
fleeing school for their holiday week
My heart, overflowing with prayers
golden healing beams of optimism
 for a resurgence of your infectious energy,

vibrant mimicry and antics.

Praying for complete restoration
of your God-given gift
 to coax reluctant smiles—
inspire joy with your beautiful musings
Please return to me
with stories of adventures,
exciting experiences
transformed into
remarkable memorable poems
A momentary escape from the dawning
of a closer-and-closer
ever-encroaching-darkness
Your dog-eared-sweating-glass-ring-smeared-pages
 of scrawled goals and dreams define
compassion, empathy, tenderness,
eloquence, humor illuminate
our heart's yearning
for our unanswered prayers.

Barely six months ago
—an unimaginable concept
a global resurgence of hope
between the cracks

of broken concrete steps

a proud green stem

with yellow petals

dancing in the summer wind

Missing your poet's

voice needing your poet's

voice pleading

to hear the ripe green treble

of your haunting poet's voice.

©Jill Sharon Kimmelman Spring 2021

Cover Design: Shamenaz
Cover Pic: Manju Yadav

पावती (स्वीकृति)

इन कविताओं के संकलन में अत्यंत धैर्य की आवश्यकता थी, जिसे मेरे माता-पिता के आशीर्वाद ने पूरा किया। इस यात्रा में मेरे बड़े भाई पंकज एवं अश्वनी, भाभी स्मिता, बड़ी बहन रंजना और उनके पति बंक बहादुर जी का बड़ा योगदान है।

इन सब के अलावा मेरे मित्र अम्बरीष, प्रदीप और उदय के सहयोग ने इस यात्रा के सफ़ल होने में योगदान दिया है।

अंततः, मैं ईश्वर के आशीर्वाद के लिए सदा आभारी रहूँगा।

अनूप कुमार

1. साहस ने साथ नहीं छोड़ा।

चाहे परिस्थितियां कितनी भी विकट क्यों न हों, चाहे मनुष्य ने कितनी ही बार पराजय का सामना क्यों न किया हो, साहस ही उसका साथ हमेशा देता है।

❧❧❧

तझड़ तो बीता नहीं अभी।
क्या बहार आएगी कभी ?
पथरीली राहें जो मिली ,
सबने मुँह फेरा तभी।
  पैरों में कांटे चुभे हुए ,
   मौसम ने भी अब मुँह मोड़ा।
   मैं थम गया कुछ क्षण तो क्या,
    साहस ने साथ नहीं छोड़ा।
"चल उठ जा, अब देर न कर",
रणभूमि से आह्वान है।
दे परिचय उस साहस का,
जिससे बैरी अंजान है।
   पर चूक गया मैं लक्ष्य से,
    फिर हार ने मुझको तोड़ा।
   समय खड़ा विपरीत तो क्या,
    साहस ने साथ नहीं छोड़ा।
हाँ, एक संदेह ने घर किया,
भय भी अब अट्टहास करे।
"विजय नहीं है अब संभव",

अंतःकरण एहसास करे।

फिर एक पुकार मन में उठी,
टूटे मन को जिसने जोड़ा।
सब छोड़ चले तो क्या हुआ,
साहस ने साथ नहीं छोड़ा।

2. यह हार भी कुछ कह जाती है ।

हमारे जीवन में जीत और हार की श्रंखला लगी रहती है। पर हमें उसे एक सबक की तरह सोचना चाहिए न कि एक अंत की तरह।

☙❧❧

यह हार भी कुछ कह जाती है,
एक आईना सा दिखाती है।
कहीं भी ना रुकना तुझे,
सबक यही सिखलाती है।
जो ठहर गया वह टूट गया,
मकसद उसका तो छूट गया।
जो रहा न कोई संग तेरे,
यह हौसला ही तेरा साथी है।

सांझ ढली तो क्या हुआ,
उम्मीद की लौ न बुझे कभी।
एक नई सहर फिर आएगी,
एक नई डगर भी लाएगी।
क्या कसर थी बाकी रह गई,
क्या कोशिश में थी कमी कोई,
क्यों खुद से ना पूछा कभी,
क्यों खुद से न पूछा कभी।

जो हैं लोगों के कहकहे,
अक्सर हम को फुसलाती हैं।
मझधारों से आगे जो बढ़े,
वही दास्तां कहलाती है।

3. भूमिपुत्र

किसान अर्थात 'भूमिपुत्र' अपने जीवन में अत्यधिक संघर्ष करता है।
उसके संघर्ष के परिणाम स्वरूप हमें भोजन मिलता है।

हो तपती धूप, या हो बदरी,
पेट भरे वो हर नगरी।
सींचे वो खेत लहू से भी,
भले वो प्यासा हो अध्-गगरी।
आभार है भूमिपुत्र का।
आभार है भूमिपुत्र का।

कभी तूफ़ान था मंडराया।
कभी आकाल का संकट छाया।
फसलें भी बेमौत मरी
पर उसने धैर्य था दिखलाया।
संघर्ष है भूमिपुत्र का।
संघर्ष है भूमिपुत्र का।

चाहे ठिठुरे वो जाड़े में,
चाहे वो झुलसे धूप में,
दुलार करे वो फ़सलों को,
ममता के हर रूप में।
दुलार है भूमिपुत्र का।
दुलार है भूमिपुत्र का।

4. वो फ़नकार क्यों अलविदा कह गया?

यह कविता भारत एवं विश्व में एक विख्यात कलाकार, श्री इरफ़ान खान जी को, जिन्हे हम ने कुछ वर्ष पहले खो दिया, एवं उनके अभिनय के लिए समर्पित है।

रूपहले परदे पे छाप थी जिसकी,
अनगिनत ही एक परिमाप थी जिसकी,
जिसने था सबको ही कायल बनाया,
जीने का हर फ़लसफ़ा था दिखाया,
  वो फ़नकार क्यों अलविदा कह गया।
  वो फ़नकार क्यों अलविदा कह गया।

नाटक हो या हो छोटा परदा,
उसने है सबको भावुक बनाया।
कभी गुदगुदाया,
कभी था रुलाया।
अभिनय भी ऐसा कि क्या भूल पाएं,
ताली औरआँसू कभी रुक न पाएं।
उसकी चमक भी कोई क्या छुपाये,
जब पश्चिम में भी उसने परचम लहराया।
हो 'मक़बूल', 'हैदर', 'चंद्रकांता' या 'हासिल',
उसका हुनर था तारीफ़ के काबिल।
कभी बाग़ी बनके बन्दूक थामी,
कभी वो दरोगा, कभी छात्र नेता।
कभी था वो क़ातिल, कभी मसखरा था ,
हर किरदार में वो हमेशा खरा था।
वो बहरूपिया अब कहाँ रुक गया ,
वो फ़नकार क्यों अलविदा कह गया।

5. लौट के तुम जो आये हो

बिजली की चमक से दी दस्तक,
है धरा भी ये नतमस्तक।
राह तेरी कब से ताके,
अब इंतज़ार भी हो कब तक।
एक झलक जो तेरी मिली,
हर चेहरे पे मुस्कान खिली।
फिर भी मन ये व्याकुल है ,
भीतर ही भीतर पूछे,
   कि लौट के तुम जो आये हो,
    बूंदों के गहने लाये हो?

जब रूठा था अम्बर हमसे,
तपती किरणों ने वार किया।
आग बबूले सूरज ने भी,
उम्मीदों का संहार किया।
ढाल बना तेरा आँचल,
और बिजली की तलवार दिखी।
घुटने टेके फ़िर दुश्मन ने,
जब बूंदों से प्रहार किया।
फिर से सवाल मन में उठे,
   कि लौट के तुम जो आये हो,
    बूंदों का तरकश लाये हो?

6. बेसब्री से इंतज़ार किया

पारा पैंतालीस पार किया,
कितनों का फिर संहार किया!
उस प्रकोप से कौन बचे ,
जब ऐसा अत्याचार किया।

धरती का आँचल सूख गया।
नदियाँ भी हँसना भूल गयी।
खेतों की हरियाली भी,
जाने कब से ग़ायब हुयी।

आसमान से किरणों ने
ताबड़तोड़ है वार किया।
काली बदरी की फौजों का
बेसब्री से इंतज़ार किया।

फ़िर काली बदरी छाई है
बूंदों की फ़ौज भी लायी है
जो भी खोया किसान ने,
ये छोटी सी भरपाई है।

तलवार चली फ़िर बिजली की,
और बाण चले हैं बूंदों के।
जब सावन सबका मीत हुआ,
तो दुश्मन भी भयभीत हुआ।

मानसून जो आया है।
संग सौग़ात भी लाया है।
न खोने का कोई ग़म रहा,
इतना जो हमने पाया है।
एक ऐसा ही उपकार किया

एक ऐसा ही उपकार किया।

7. नयी डगर

उम्र गुज़रती रहती है,
फिर वक़्त फ़िसलता रहता है।
कितना अब और भी लड़ना है,
मन ये सवाल फ़िर करता है।

कुछ शिकस्त हम पाए हैं।
हाँ, चोट भी अक्सर खाए हैं।
नाकामियों से रचा हुआ,
इतिहास भी हम दोहराए हैं।

पर क्या हम सचमुच हार चुके ?
क्या कभी नहीं होगी सहर ?
क्यों लगे किअब अँधेरा है ?
क्या नहीं दिखेगी नयी पहर ?

इतिहास तो हम दोहराते हैं।
फिर भूल ये कैसे जाते हैं ?
हर किसी के बीते पलों में भी,
कुछ यादग़ार सौगातें हैं।
क्यों न पलटें उन पन्नों को,
जिनमें वो यादें रहती हैं,
है ज़िन्दगी बेरंग नहीं,
जो ये बातें भी कहती हैं।
इतिहास भी उनको पूजता है,
जिसने है खोया सब कुछ।
पर हार न जिसने मानी है,

है योद्धा वो ही सचमुच ।

अपनी भी दौलत हिम्मत है।
है अपने साथ जो ये अगर,
हर बादल फिर छट जाएगा,
फिर दिखेगी हमको नयी डगर।

8. बस इतना हासिल कर लूं

यह कविता एक ऐसे व्यक्ति की मनोदशा को व्यक्त करती है, जो भ्रष्ट आचरण कारण कारावास की सजा काट रहा है और जिसे अपने भ्रष्ट आचरण के कारण हुए हादसे का पश्चाताप है।

क नयी सुबह की दस्तक थी,
ये क़ायनात नतमस्तक थी,
एक नया पड़ाव था जीवन का,
खुशियों की कहानी तब तक थी।
फिलहाल कहानी ऐसी है,
जैसे बिन पंख परिन्दा हूँ।
अँधेरी चार दीवारी में,
बीते लम्हों संग ज़िंदा हूँ।

मूंदी हुयी आँखें कहती हैं
मैं आसमान में फ़िर उड़ लूँ।
एक नयी ऊंचाई फिर चूमूँ।
एक नयी ऊंचाई फिर चूमूँ।

ख्वाबों के लाखों रंगों में,
फिर ख़ुद को ज़ाहिर कर लूँ।
बस इतना हासिल कर लूं।
बस इतना हासिल कर लूं।

थी ज़िद एक आगे बढ़ने की,
एक नए शिखर पे चढ़ने की।
मेरा गुरूर हमराह हुआ।
जाने कब मैं गुमराह हुआ !

कितने ही घर बर्बाद हुए
मेरी इस ज़िद की हुकूमत से।
थी चादर मेरी छोटी पर
माँगा अधिक ज़रुरत से।

दिखता बस एक अँधेरा है।
लगता नाराज़ सवेरा है।
सन्नाटों के साये में
रोता हर ख़्वाब ये मेरा है।

अब हिम्मत न बची है कि,
टूटे सपनों को जोड़ सकूँ।
अपने बेबस इन हाथों से
जीवन की कश्ती मोड़ सकूँ।

भूल के अपना बीता कल,
फिर से एक आग़ाज़ करू।
खुद को इस काबिल कर लूँ।
बस इतना हासिल कर लूं।
बस इतना हासिल कर लूं।

9. हारेगा नहीं तू इस युग में

कुछ सिक्कों की खनक में जब,

कुछ सफ़ेदपोश बईमान हुए,

अपनी जेबें भरने के लिए

किस हद तक वे ऐसे नादान हुए,

जब नए सुबह की उम्मीदों के,

ओझल सारे अरमान हुए,

है इंसानियत का चेहरा क्या,

इस बात सब अंजान हुए,

एक तू ही था जिसे थी फ़िकर

आने वाली सदियों के लिए।

क्यों डरता है कि अकेला ही

क्या अपनी मंज़िल पाएगा !

है तूने जो आग़ाज़ किया,

तूफानों से लड़ जाएगा।

तेरे ही बदौलत है बची,

हम सब में कुछ उम्मीदें हैं।

हैं सब की सदाएं संग तेरे,

हर किले को फतह कर जाएगा।

लेकर फिर सुबह का उजियारा

अध्याय रचेगा कलियुग में।

टूटेगा नहीं तू इस युग में।

हारेगा नहीं तू इस युग में।

10. जल का मरहम

भोर से निकला हुआ मुसाफ़िर,
बुझ कर जैसे बेहाल हुआ।
इस मुरझाये से चेहरे पे,
खुशियों का जो आकाल हुआ।
था हरियाली का साया जो,
वो न तो अबकी साल हुआ।
फसलें जो अब चौपट हुयी,
फिर किसान कंगाल हुआ।

अम्बर को निहारते रहते कि
तपता सूरज थक जायेगा।
नीला सा दिखता साया ये,
बादलों से फिर ढक जाएगा।

धरती हमसे अब ख़फ़ा हुयी,
जैसे हमसे कोई ख़ता हुयी।
आँसुओं से खेतों को सींचा,
नदियां जो अब लापता हुयी।
बारिश को तरसें हम बेबस,
पर बादलों की है आँख-मिचौली।
देकर खुशियों का ये झांसा,
लौटें लेकर अपनी टोली।

जो इंतेज़ार है सावन का,
जाने किस हद तक जाएगा!
धरती के आँचल में बादल,
जल का मरहम रख जाएगा।

11. ऐसी हो कल की सुबह

हूँ बैठा मैं इंतज़ार में,
कि वो दिन भी आएगा,
जब देकर सब को ही खुशियाँ,
ये दिन यूँ ही ढल जाएगा।
खिलते फूलों जैसे ही,
सबके चेहरे खिलने लगें।
मुस्कुराहटों की आस में,
अपनी नींदों से हम जगें।

और हमें मिले जीने की वजह।
ऐसी हो कल की सुबह।

सोते हुए सपनें बोलें कि,
अब और न इनको सोना है।
मैले कल की चादर में नहीं,
एक नए लिबास में होना है।
हर फतह की दावेदार ये,
अपनी राहों में चल पड़ें।
उम्मीदें हैं जो इनसे जुड़ी,
इन्हें साकार ही होना है।

दे इन्हें आगे बढ़ने की ज़िरह,
ऐसी हो कल की सुबह।

12. आँखें न मूंदो मेरी अभी

कुछ सपने देखने दो मुझे।
कुछ तो मुझे आगे बढ़ने दो।
आख़र क्या है क्या पता मुझे,
कुछ तो पन्ने मुझे पढ़ने दो।

क्या खुशबुएँ हैं बाग़ों में,
न मैं उनसे रूबरू हुयी।
क्या कह गयी हवा मुझसे,
मेरी न ही गुफ़्तगू हुयी।
मेरे इस राह में काँटे तो,
हैं बिछाए जो दुश्मन सभी।
कि मैं इनमें अब उबर सकूँ,
आँखें न मूंदो मेरी अभी।

क्यों है ये डर कि तू सोचे,
न जी सकूंगी मैं और यहाँ,
जो न महफ़ूज़ मैं तेरे आंचल में,
हूँ महफ़ूज़ मैं और कहाँ ?
हैं जिन्होंने सब दस्तूर लिखे,
क्या हैसियत है उन सब की?

कि है दूबर जीना मेरा,
छूटी ये सोच जाने कब की।
क्यों लगता है कि दूजे दर पे,
न मिलेगा तेरा प्यार कभी ?
कि ख़ोज सकूँ मैं ऐसा प्यार,
आँखें न मूंदो मेरी अभी।

13. है यही दास्तां अंधेरे की

सब कुछ ही खो गया है जिसमें,
पहचान सो गयी है जिसमें,
अस्तित्व नहीं जहाँ रंगों का,
जहाँ छोर दिखे न अंगों का,
हमदर्द जो गुनहगारों का,
कोख़ है काले कारोबारों का,
निगली जिसने परछाई है,
बुनता है जो ख़्वाब हज़ारों का,
माशूख है चोर-लुटेरे की।
है यही दास्तां अंधेरे की।

जिसमें हैं घुले से रंग कई,
सदियां भी जिसमें डूब गयी।
रौशनी से जिसकी रंजिश है।
इससे ही उबरना ख़्वाहिश है।
इसकी गहराई के भीतर,
कुछ राज़ भी छिपकर रहते हैं,
जिनका सच कभी न खुल सका,
ऐसा कुछ लोग भी कहते हैं।

एक नयी शुरुआत सवेरे की।
है यही दास्तां अंधेरे की।

14. मेरी ख़ामियाँ

जो पर मेरे टूटे हैं अब
बिखरा हुआ लगता है सब।
अलफ़ाज़ भी हैं खो गए,
जिन्हें ढूंढते हैं मेरे लब।
भूला हूँ मैं उस शख़्स को
जो साथ मेरे था यहाँ।
जो मुझमें ही कहीं छुपा था
जिसे मिटा सका न ये जहां।
कोसों आगे मैं बढ़ गया
पीछे हैं फ़िर भी खींचती
मेरी ख़ामियाँ।
मेरी ख़ामियाँ।

क़ाबिलियत जो थी मेरी
उन सब को ये दफ़ना गयी।
नाकामियों के दाग़ को,
हैं जैसे ये अपना गयी।
क्या था हासिल जिसे भुला चुका
है ख़ोज मुझे जिसकी कबसे?
न इल्म कि कब मैं उभरूँगा
मायूसियों के इस रब से?
हूँ मैं भी इनका साझेदार
जिन्हें ढोती हैं मेरे साथ ये
मेरी ख़ामियाँ।
मेरी ख़ामियाँ।

हर बार हूँ मैं ये सोचता,
कि कब ये पीछा छोड़ेंगी ?
बिखरा हूँ मैं तो सदियों से,
मुझे और ये कितना तोड़ेंगी ?
आने वाले हैं नए पल,
ऐसा गुमां हुआ है मुझे।
इस पल में बला ये छूटेगी,
इस सोच ने छुआ है मुझे।
[अ]ग़र इन्हे याद न मैं रहूँ
और ये पीछे न मुड़ी कभी,
ख़ुद से पूछूंगा कहाँ गयी ?
मेरी ख़ामियाँ।
मेरी ख़ामियाँ।

15. तेरा वजूद भी होना है

[अ]ग़र बयां करूँ ये दास्तां,
हूँ तेरा शुक्रगुज़ार मैं।
जो शिकश्त को पीछे छोड़ा तो,
तुझपे हँसता हर बार मैं।
अपनों की दुआएं साथ थी,
पर उन सब से भी थी बढ़कर,
तेरी रंजिश जो मुझसे थी
किया जिसका सामना मैं डंटकर।

जो मौके तुझको थे मिले,
उन्हें खोने का तेरा रोना है।
मेरे मक़सद को पाने में,
तेरा वजूद भी होना है।

था वक़्त भी तुझको खूब मिला,
कि मुझे मात तू दे सके।
फ़िर तूने साजिश रची ऐसी
जिससे कि मेरी रूह थके।
जब सफ़र की एक पगडण्डी पे,
मैं गिर गया बेसुध हो कर,
तुझे हुयी ग़लतफ़हमी ये कि,
हारूँगा मैं सबकुछ खोकर।

जो उठकर खड़ा हुआ फ़िर से,
तेरे होश तो जैसे उड़ गये।
मेरे साहस के टूटे पर,
जैसे अब फ़िर से जुड़ गये।
तेरी चकाचौंध फ़ीकी पड़ी।

काहे का अब तू सोना है।
तेरी हार के इस किस्से में
तेरा वजूद भी होना है।

हम एक जगह से शुरु हुए,
पर तू आगे था निकल गया।
हारा न मैं हिम्मत फ़िर भी,
और लाया अन्दर जोश नया।
तू मुड़कर जो देखा तो,
कोई फ़ासला अब न दिखा।
तुझसे आगे न निकल सकूँ,
इस सोच में तेरा अक्स बिका।

तूने कांटे थे कई बिछाए,
अपनी शिकश्त के हर डर से।
पर मैं करीब हूँ मंज़िल के,
जिसे पाने को अब तू तरसे।
खेला तू अपने वक़्त से,
जैसे कोई नया खिलौना है
मेरे इस जीत कि मजलिस में,
तेरा वजूद भी होना है।

16. थी जिसकी वो हक़दार सदा

थी सदियों से उसकी पुकार
कि उसको अपना हक़ मिले।
इस संघर्ष में थी आहत,
न किसी ने उसके ज़ख़्म सिले।
उसकी हर मांग के बदले में,
थे हर सितम उसके लिए।
थे ज़ख्म जो भी उसको मिले,
आंसुओं ने उसको बयां किए।
पर आंसुओं को पोछती,
हक़ के लिए लड़ती रही।
लांघ के हर दहलीज वो
आगे ही बढ़ती रही।

टूटे न उसके हौसले
और पा लिया उसने वो सब,
थी जिसकी वो हक़दार सदा।
थी जिसकी वो हक़दार सदा।

थी बंद इकलौते कमरे में।
न घूंघट उसका हटा कभी।
पर उसके माथे के तेज से,
न अंधेरा टिका कभी।
न किसी ने सोचा था कभी,
कि आसमां वो छू लेगी।

और प्रजातंत्र के हर तपके को
उसका सारा अब हक़ देगी।
अंतरिक्ष में जाकर उसने,
कुछ रहस्य भी सुलझाए थे।
और कभी बेघर बच्चों पे,
उसने आँचल फैलाये थे।

जो था सैलाब आंसुओं का
फिर भी डाली कश्ती अपनी।
घूंघट से बना के आसमां,
बसा गयी बस्ती अपनी।

फ़िर रुका न उसका काफ़िला,
और जीत लिया उसने वो सब
थी जिसकी वो हक़दार सदा।
थी जिसकी वो हक़दार सदा।

17. क्योंकि...

न मंदिर मैं गया कभी,
न ही सजदे में झुका कभी।
औरों का देखा देखी भी,
मन की करने में न रुका कभी।

क्योंकि न मैला है मन मेरा
न कभी बुरा ये करता है।
देखे जो किसी का दर्द ये,
उसका हर ज़ख्म ये भरता है।

थे पाखण्डी तो बहुतेरे,
करते थे ढोंग मानवता का।
करते थे इबादत मतलब से
ठगते थे भरोसा जनता का।
देते मूरत को वो आहार,
औरों पे थी उनकी फ़टकार।
न था उनके मन में कभी
कि वो करें सबका उद्धार।

न पता था मुझे कि क्या रखूं
मानवता का पैमाना मैं।
है कहाँ धूल में लिपटी ये,
ढूंढूं सारा तहख़ाना मैं।

क्योंकि थी ज़रुरत एक ऐसी
जो सबने महसूस किया।
थी तोड़नी वो मनमानी
जिसने सदियों से हुकुम किया।

18. कुछ ऐसे अलविदा कहूँ

भ्रम था कि मैं हूँ जी रहा
ये ज़िन्दगी अपने लिए।
पर ज़िन्दगी मुझे जी रही थी
अपना मकसद पाने के लिए।
जो भ्रम है टूटा,
फिर मैं समझा,
कि मैं तो ज़रिया मात्र था,
मुस्कुराहटें लाने के लिए।
जो हो गया मकसद ये पूरा,
मुझको है बुलाती मौत अब
किसी और के जीने के लिए।

अब जो आंसू छलके तो,
इन आंसुओं में मैं दिखूं।
न भुला सके ये दौर मुझे,
कुछ ऐसे अलविदा कहूँ।
कुछ ऐसे अलविदा कहूँ।

कुछ रोज़ पहले हुआ गुमान
कि चंद लम्हे हैं बचे।
इनको मैं कैसे जियूं,
ये बवाल अब फिर मचे।
क्या मैं जियूं ख़ुद के लिए,
या फिर जियूं उनके लिए,
जिनकी सारी उम्मीदों ने

हर कदम पे मेरा साथ दिए।
जाना था दुनियां को देकर,
अपनी वो सारी दौलतें,
जिन्हें न कभी लुटा सका,
जो थी थोड़ी ही मोहलतें।

धूल जमे मेरी कब्र पे,
पर यादों पे जमने न दूं।
जीना चाहे मुझे ज़िन्दगी,
कुछ ऐसे अलविदा कहूँ।
कुछ ऐसे अलविदा कहूँ।

19. फ़िर कोई क्यों ये न कहे

तन्हा सूनी गलियों में कभी,
जब भी उसकी आहट सुनी,
झपटे उसपे कुछ भेड़िये,
फ़िर भी न किसी ने चीख सुनी।

थी गुहार उसकी सबसे,
कि कोई तो हाथ बढ़ा सके।
पर सब अपने मतलब में डूबे,
अपनी एक अलग ही राह चुनी।

जो ये हालात हैं शहरों में,
फ़िर कोई क्यों ये न कहे,
इससे बेहतर तो बीहड़ है।
रखते हैं मूरत देवी की,
घर-घर में पूजा करते हैं।
पर बाहर समाज में ही,
उसको ही सताया करते हैं।

जब कभी मोहल्ले से गुज़रे,
सब ऐसे घूरते हैं उसको,
जैसे उनके घरवालों ने
दी खुली छूट है इन सब की।
फ़िर क्यों हैं ढोंग वो करते कि
नारी ही उनकी देवी है !
और उन्ही से उनकी भक्ति है।

रखें जो फ़रेबी हर चेहरा
और ढोंग रचें वो भक्ति का,
फ़िर कोई क्यों ये न कहे

हम जैसा ढोंगी और नहीं।

20. क्या पता कि...

एक दिन ऐसे ही इत्तेफ़ाक़ से
एक मोड़ पे एक राही से मिला
लगता था जो हारा हुआ
जिसे ज़िन्दगी से था ग़िला।
वो पहुँच गया उस मोड़ पे
जहां हर उम्मीदें गुम हुयी।
ग़म के कई थपेड़ों से
उसकी आँखें भी नम हुयी।
उसने माना कुछ रहा नहीं,
अब अलविदा कहने के सिवा।
अलविदा उस ज़िन्दगी को
जिसकी क़ीमत वो न समझा।

उसको समझाया मैंने कि
हर दिन एक जैसा तो नहीं।
क्या पता कि कल उसे वो मिले
जिसका था वो हक़दार रहा।

मैंने उसको बतलाया कि
फ़िर मिलेंगे मौक़े और भी।
बनके विजेता वो उभरे,
आएगा ऐसा दौर भी।
जो छोड़ दी जीने कि डगर,
तो ये मौक़ा भी छूटेगा।
मानके तुझको ही कायर

ये जहां भी तुझसे रूठेगा।
रह जायेगी हावी वो वजह
जिसने तुझको मजबूर किया।
हार के जिससे अब तूने,
ख़ुद को जीने से दूर किया।

क्या हुआ जो न कोई साथ दे,
तू ख़ुद को ही साथी कहे।
न सोच तू अगले जनम की,
क्या पता कि कैसा जनम रहे !

उसमें मैंने ख़ुद को देखा
और फ़िर मुझको एहसास हुआ
कि मेरे जीवन से भी ज्यादा
ये ग़म औरों का ख़ास हुआ।
ये बात उसे समझाया मैंने
और उसको एक राह दिखायी
न वो पीछे मुड़ देखे,
जीने की ऐसी चाह सिखायी।
जो खुशियाँ उसको हैं मिली,
और जो रिश्ते उससे हैं जुड़े,
उन सब कि ख़ातिर है जीना
संग जिनके उसकी हर राह मुड़े।

क्यों छोड़ के सारी खुशियों को
और छोड़ के सारे रिश्तों को
तूने ऐसी है डगर चुनी,
जहाँ पे इनकी खबर नहीं।

क्या पता कि जो भी है मिला
जिनको पाकर तू खुश रहा,
न हों नसीब अगले जनम।
न हों नसीब अगले जनम।

21. फ़िर से हिन्दुस्तान उठा

यह कविता इसरो (ISRO) के मंगलयान की सफ़ल उड़ान एवं उपलब्धि पर केंद्रित है।

देखा सपना सदियों से कि,
अंतरिक्ष में जाना है।
क्या क्या है छुपा इस अम्बर में,
इसका जवाब भी पाना है।
सदियों से कैद था कमरे में,
फ़िर भी उम्मीदें न खोयी।
तयं कर लिया कि ये ब्रह्माण्ड,
ही उसका नया ठिकाना है।
भुला के फ़िर बीते कल को
और तोड़ के अपनी हर बेड़ी,
फ़िर से हिन्दुस्तान उठा।

थे राह में कुछ कांटे बिछे
जिनसे जूझे आगे बढ़ा।
और एक दिन आया फ़िर ऐसा
कि आसमां पे ये चढ़ा।
रखा इसने ऐसा दर्पण,
जिसमें सारी धरती दिखें।
थी चाँद को छूने की इच्छा,
अब उस मक़सद पे ये अड़ा।
इक्कीसवीं सदी में आ के

अपना परचम लहराने को,
फिर से हिन्दुस्तान उठा।

देखा चाँद पे इसने जल,
जब चंद्रयान की थी सवारी।
नयी जगह जीवन के लिए,
मंगल पे जाने की तैयारी।
ख़ुद पे निर्भर रहने के लिए
इसने अपनी तकनीक चुनी।

पर कुछ असफ़ल प्रयासों से
इसने खेली अपनी पारी।

मायूस हुआ
पर न टूटा।
अपने मकसद पे फिर जुटा।
अब कि अपने हौसले के बूते
ख़ुद को इसने साबित किया।
इस हौसले के सहारे ,
नभ में अपनी कश्ती उतारे,
फिर से हिन्दुस्तान उठा।
अपना हिंदुस्तान उठा।

22. तू तो योद्धा है सदियों का

पहला जो कदम था युद्ध में तेरा,
न थी दुश्मन के वार की आहट।
फ़िर भी तूने अपने दम पे,
दी उसको एक कड़ी चुनौती।
जो हाथ से छूटे युद्ध ये तेरे,
क़ाबिलियत की है एक और कसौटी।

हैं ज़ख्म तेरे अभी भरे नहीं।
पर तू अभी तो टूटा ही नहीं।
तू तो योद्धा है सदियों का
तेरी अगली कसौटी है यही।

तेरी हार को दुश्मन ने माना
कि ये तेरी कमजोरी है।
इसलिए तेरी गलतियों को भाँपे,
उसने कोई राह न छोड़ी है।
तू हौसले को कर बुलंद
और फ़िर से अपनी राह चुन।
जो गूँज है तेरे ख़िलाफ़
अनसुनी कर ऐसी हर धुन।

जो कदम हैं आगे को बढ़े,
फ़िर न आगे कोई सोच अड़े।
तू तो योद्धा है सदियों का,
जो अधर्म के विपरीत लड़े।

बीती हुयी अपनी ग़लती को
तू भूल के आगे चल निकला।

क्या बात है तेरी मेहनत से
अब तो हर पत्थर है पिघला !
पर तेरी रफ़्तार से अब
एक लहर है ऐसी फ़ैल गयी,
कि तेरे हर दुश्मन ने,
फ़िर तुझको ललकारा है।
आगे क्या है अंजाम तेरा,
क्यों तू परवाह करता उसकी ?
तू तो योद्धा है सदियों का
हर सदी में एक पहचान है जिसकी।

23. फ़िर भी...

थे ग़म के पहरे फ़ैले हुए,
जिनसे न रूबरू पहले हुए।
जो थी चाहत मुस्कानों की तो
खुशियों के अरमां मैले हुए।
फिर भी न ही अफ़सोस किया।
और आंसुओं को सम्भाला मैंने।
क्योंकि थी मुश्किलें और खड़ी।
क्योंकि थी मुश्किलें और खड़ी।

जो थे उमीदों के बादल
उनसे न कोई बात बनी।
आगे बढ़ने की ज़िद से फ़िर
थी औरों से जंग ठनी।
फ़िर भी हम सम्भाले हिम्मत को,
अक्सर आगे बढ़ते ही रहे।
क्योंकि मेरा रस्ता देखे
थी राहें कुछ और खड़ी।
थी राहें कुछ और खड़ी।

था आसरा जिनसे राहत का
विश्वास का उन्होंने ग़बन किया।
उनको लगता कि मेरी खुशियों को
उन्होंने है एक कफ़न दिया।
वो थे कल ग़लत और आज भी हैं।
फ़िर भी उनकी इस नादानी को,
हम नज़रअंदाज़ हैं करते
क्योंकि मेरे सपनों ने फ़िर

कुछ और भी खुशियां हैं बुनी।
कुछ और भी खुशियां हैं बुनी।

24. कमी न थी

यूँ तो आगे बढ़ते रहे,
पर राहों की कोई कमी न थी।
साजिश करते तूफानों की
अभी रफ़्तार थमी न थी।
गिरते भी रहे पर न थमे,
ये कदम कभी जो न जमे।
न रुके कभी।
चलते रहे।
तपती धूपों में
ढलते रहे।

मेरे ज़ख्मों पे लहू भी थे,
और आँखों में नमी भी थी।
पर जो आगे लेकर चलें,
उन मुस्कुराहटों की कमी न थी।

फ़िर हुआ सामना सच से कि
ख़ुद राह भी अपनी चुननी है।
मैं लाख करूं फ़रियाद वफ़ा की
न किसी को मेरी सुननी है।
जो रोक सकें मुझको अक्सर,
ऐसे अब मोड़ मिलेंगे यहाँ।
कि थाम सकें वो कदम मेरे,
ऐसी ही जाल उन्हें बुननी हैं।
संग चलते क़दमों की अक्सर,
आहटों की कमी भी थी।
पर कुछ दुआओं में लिपटी,

उन राहतों की कमी न थी।

25. क्या उसकी गलती थी कि

उसने था सुना कि पढ़ने को,
बस था आखर का ज्ञान जरूरी।
पर उसकी छोटी जाति ने ही,
रखी उसकी इच्छा ये अधूरी।
था उसके घर का सपना कि
वो अपने घर का चिराग बने।
पर जाति की अड़चन ने चाहा कि
वो दुनिया पे दाग बने।

जब न सच हो सका वो सपना,
फिर उसने खुद से पूछा कि
क्या उसकी गलती थी कि
उसने इस घर में जन्म लिया।

इसकी श्रद्धा थी मिलने की उसे,
जिसे सब पूजा करते थे।
पर उस दर पे जाने को तो,
सब जाति ही पूछा करते थे।
मिल न सका वो कभी उससे,
जिसने रचना की सृष्टि की।
पर क्यों उससे है भेद भाव,
न किसी ने इसकी पुष्टि की।

कभी सपने में जो प्रभु मिले,
उनसे इसने फिर पूछा कि
क्या उसकी गलती थी कि
वो जन्मा उसकी इस श्रृष्टि में।
हम सबको पता वो गलत नहीं,

फिर क्यों उसको ऐसे देखें कि
जैसे उसने गलती की है,
जन्म लेकर के उस जाति में।

क्यों उसको मजबूर करें,
कि वो सोचे अब ऐसा कि
क्या उसकी गलती थी कि
वो जन्मा हम इंसानों में।

26. पर थी किसको परवाह मेरी

यह कविता उस पल को बयां करती है जब पंछी वापस आकर अपना घोसला उजड़ा हुआ पाता है। उसे यह पता है कि सब एक प्राकृतिक त्रासदी का परिणाम है। पर इस त्रासदी के पीछे मनुष्य की लापरवाही हुयी है। लापरवाही, प्रकृति के प्रति और लापरवाही जीव जन्तुवों के प्रति। परन्तु क्या ये इससे सबक लेगा ?

જ જ જ

जब लौट के अपने घर आया,
मिला टूटा सपनों का किला।
ढूँढा मैंने फिर अपनों को,
न पता ठिकाना उनका मिला।
कुछ इंसानों कि बस्ती भी,
उजड़ी हुयी सी मुझे दिखी।
और उम्मीद कि किरणें भी,
धुंधली-धुंधली सी मुझे दिखी।
उन्होंने फिर से जोड़ के सब,
अपना आशियाना खड़ा किया।
पर उन सब ने न पूछा कि
अब मेरा फिर क्या होगा।
मैंने भी बहुत कुछ खोया था।
अपनों से बिछड़ के रोया था।
कुछ अश्क़ों ने मेरे भी,
उजड़ी धरती को भिगोया था।
पर थी किसको परवाह मेरी।

पर थी किसको परवाह मेरी।

वो कहते हैं कि उन्होंने भी,
अपनों की जान गंवायी है।
कैसे वो दें अब मुझे आसरा,
जब उनकी जान पे आई है।
वो कहते हैं कि मैं काबिल हूँ,
कि फ़िर परवाज़ें भर सकूँ।
तिनकों को जोड़ के फ़िर से मैं,
अपना घर खड़ा मैं कर सकूँ।

पर अब मुझ में है कहाँ वो हिम्मत,
कि मैं टूटे को जोड़ सकूँ।
जो मुझे छोड़ कर चले गए,
कैसे उनका रुख मोड़ सकूँ।
जो ये धरती अब उजड़ी है,
उनकी है इसमें जिम्मेदारी।
जो इनका था फ़र्ज़ यहाँ,
उससे की इन्होने ग़द्दारी।

थक हार गया कह के उनसे,
कि कुदरत का सम्मान करें।
अपने मतलब के लिए कभी
न कल का फ़िर अपमान करें।
पर थी किसको परवाह मेरी।
पर थी किसको परवाह मेरी।

27. तेरी सख्शियत इकलौती है

बीते कल ने खो दिया तुझे,
उसका एक यही तो रोना है।
आने वाले कल को डर है,
कि उसे भी तुझको खोना है।
सब की नज़र थी बस तुझपे ही,
सब तुझसे आस लगाते थे।
तेरी एक झलक के लिए,
सबकुछ ही दावं लगाते थे ।

तू जब उतरा लेकर के अस्त्र
सबको ही दिया चुनौती है।

तुझसा नहीं दूजा है योद्धा
तेरी सख़िशयत इकलौती है।

जो हार गया तुझसे कभी,
न उसे अफ़सोस है हार का।
उसे गर्व है कि उसने है किया,
सामना तेरे प्रहार का।
चाहे हो तेरी छोटी सी काया,
चाहे छोटी परछाईं हो,
तूने हैं वार झेले सभी,
चाहे कोई फ़ौज भी आयी हो।

तूने जो अस्त्र है त्याग दिया,
ये युद्ध भूमि अब रोती है।
तुझपे सदैव गौरव रहे,
ये सपने सदा संजोती है।
ये सपने सदा संजोती है।

28. फिर लौट के वापस आउंगा

अश्क़ों में डूबे घर से ख़त,
मुझसे मिलने की इक आफ़त,
छोटी बहना की हर एक शरारत,
और होली पे मुझे रंगने की आदत,
हर एक ने ज़िक्र किया यही
हर एक ने फिक्र किया यही
कि क्या मैं यहाँ सलामत हूँ।

हर ज़िक्र को मैं फ़िर सुनकर
हर फ़िक्र को करके दर-किनार,
छुपा के अपनी हर मजबूरी
और पोंछ के आँसू फिर अपने
करता सबसे झूठा वादा कि,
रंगने होली की रंगत में
फिर लौट के वापस आउंगा।

घर पे बैठी उस माँ को भी,
पता है कि मैं न आउंगा।
जो वो नाराज़ हो झूठ से मेरे,
उसे हर मजबूरी बताऊंगा।
इस माँ का दिल तो टूट गया
उस माँ कि लाज बचाने में।
पिता को मेरे गर्व है मुझपे
ग़म है उन्हें मेरे न आने में।

ताकि उन दिलों को जोड़ सकूँ
और हर नाराज़गी तोड़ सकूँ
देता हूँ दिलासा दिवाली का

और फिर उन सब से कहता हूँ,
रौशन करने अपने घर को
फिर लौट के वापस आउंगा।

जैसे कि उनको पता था
कि मैं न फिर आ पाउँगा।
वो हो गए नाराज़ मुझसे
सोचे मैं उन्हें मनाऊंगा।
पर उनको है न पता
कि मैं किस हाल में हूँ यहाँ।
मैं लड़ रहा हूँ इस सरहद पे
जीते हर पहर ही मौत जहाँ।

उनका भी कहना ज़ायज है
उनसे मिले हुआ एक अरसा।
अपने हर फ़र्ज़ को निभा लिया
फिर भी मैं उनके साथ को तरसा।
पर मैंने ये तयं है किया
कि चाहे मुझको अब मौत मिले
पर लिपटा हुआ तिरंगे में
फिर लौट के वापस आउंगा।

29. रखूँगा कदम इस धरती पे

ये कल्पना है उस समय कि जब मानवता एक युद्ध के कग़ार पे आ गयी है। और इस कुरुक्षेत्र का योद्धा अब विनती करता है कि प्रभु फिर से धरती पे आयें और मानवता का परचम लहराएं।

❧ ❧ ❧

जब आसमां को छू के भी,
फ़ितरत रह जाए गिरी हुयी
जब धन-दौलत के नशे में ही,
ये क़ायनात सरफिरी हुयी ।

जब उम्मीदों के लौ से भी,
ग़मों कि कालिख न उतरे
सुनकर आग़ाज़ बर्बादी की,
जब इंसानियत भी न सुधरे
सुनने को तेरी हर दुआ,
रखूँगा कदम इस धरती पे।
रखूँगा कदम इस धरती पे।

जब देख के तेरे आँसू भी,
मानवता कभी न पिघले
तू हो ऐसे असमंजस में'
कि आगे कोई न हल निकले

होकर मलंग झूठे वादों से
सब कसमें-रसमें तोड़ गए,

कि हरा सकें एक दूजे को,
नैतिक मूल्यों को छोड़ गए
नैतिकता का परचम लहराने
रखूँगा कदम इस धरती पे।
रखूँगा कदम इस धरती पे।
इस युद्ध का तू ही एक योद्धा
और मैं खुद तेरी सेना हूँ
कि हरा सके तू दुश्मन को
तुझको तरकश ये उठाना है
मेरा कर्तव्य इस कुरुक्षेत्र में
तुझको सही मार्ग दिखाना है।
उठा ले तू गांडीव अब
और शंख बजा दे युद्ध का
मानवता को फिर विजयी करने
मैं जन्मा हूँ इस धरती पे।
मैं जन्मा हूँ इस धरती पे।

30. क्रांति की गूँज

अपनी धरती आज़ाद है और
हम आज़ाद मुल्क़ के वासी हैं,
फिर अपने दिल में क्यों पलती
एक डर और एक उदासी हैं ।

कहाँ गयी वो सोच जिसे हम,
आधारशिला कहलाते थे?
एक नयी सुबह की देख झलकियाँ,
सब अपना मन बहलाते थे ।
कहते थे हम लड़ जायेंगे
वो अस्सी या इक्क्यासी हैं ।

क्रांति की इस सोच को
तुम जंग न लगने देना कभी,
ये तेरा हथियार है राही।
ये तेरा हथियार है राही।
तोड़ दे तू इस चक्रव्यूह को
क्रांति की है ये गूँज सिपाही।

इस भ्रष्ट तन्त्र से मुक्ति पाने को
कुछ और भी सदियाँ प्यासी हैं।

31. कुछ दूर अभी चलना है मुझे

जब भी ये कदम बढ़ते हैं मेरे,
ये वक़्त भी आगे बढ़ता है।
जो था सोया सा एक सूरज,
फिर आसमान में चढ़ता है।
बरसात की जो कुछ बूँदें है,
और चकाचौंध जो किरणे हैं।
ये मुझे अब कहती हैं
कि

"कुछ दूर अभी चलना है मुझे
कुछ दूर अभी चलना है मुझे"

जिस रस्ते पे चलना था मुझे,
उसके थे निशां मिटे हुए।
जो मंज़िल करनी थी हासिल,
उसके थे लाखों राही दिखे।
अपनी राहें फिर बना लिया,
और चुना एक नया सा कारवां।
पर सही राह तय करने के लिए,
कुछ दूर अभी चलना है मुझे।
कुछ दूर अभी चलना है मुझे।

मैं खड़ा हूँ अब उस मोड़ पे कि,
मेरी हर शक्ति ख़तम हुयी।
पर मुझको इस दूरी से,
दिखती नज़दीक वो मंजिल है।
पर उस तक चलने के लिए,

ताकि उसका दर चूम सकूँ,
कुछ दूर अभी चलना है मुझे।
कुछ दूर अभी चलना है मुझे।

32. बिछड़ा चेहरा

आगे की होड़ में ही कहीं,
एक भाग-दौड़ में ही कहीं,
मुझे छोड़ गया कब खबर नहीं,
फिर ढूँढू क्या उसे वहीं।

बिछड़ा चेहरा।
बिछड़ा चेहरा।
न मिला कभी,
बिछड़ा चेहरा।

जब निकला मैं अपने घर से,
तब से वो मेरे साथ ही था।
फिर नए शहर में जब आया,
हर किसी को चेहरा रास नहीं।
पर इस नादान के सिवा,
था कोई भी दूजा पास नहीं।

जब मिलता था मक्कारों से,
उनको इसने बइमान कहा।
पर इस नादान को क्या पता,
कि उन्हें नापसंद है सच्चाई।
फिर भी ये मूरख न सुधरा,
इसने हर सच की कीमत चुकाई।

मैं लड़ बैठा इस चेहरे से,
जिसने न सीखी थी चतुराई।
फिर छोड़ के जो ये चला गया,
कभी भी इसकी खबर न आयी।

बाँध के तानों की गठरी,
कहाँ गुम हुआ मेरा चेहरा।
फिर मिला नहीं बिछड़ा चेहरा।
फिर मिला नहीं बिछड़ा चेहरा।

33. कहता ये अलविदा सावन है

हफ़्तों पहले की बात थी जब,
तू ने दी दस्तक ख़बरों से।
सब निहारते रहे आसमां,
पुष्प भी पूछे भवरों से,
कि कब तू आएगा मेरे आँगन,
उम्मीदों के शहरों से।
मुक्त करेगा धरती को,
सूखे-आकाल के पहरों से।

फिर तू आया,
खुशियाँ लाया।
खेतों में दिखी,
खुशियों की छाया।
और अब तेरी ही बदौलत,
बूंदों से भरा फिर आँगन है।
बूंदों से भरा फिर आँगन है।

तू सबका मेहमान था,
पर तू ने की ख़ातिरदारी।
कुछ पल तू सबके साथ रहा,
फिर वापस जाने की तैयारी।
चाहे ये आसमां कि तू ठहरे।
फिर है ये गुज़ारिश लहरों की
कहीं और न जा अब तू रुक जा।
ये दुआ है साँझ-दोपहरों की।

पर अब तुझको जाना ही है।
कहीं और है तेरा इंतज़ार।
जो न पहुँचा तू वहाँ अगर,
वो रहेंगे फिर तो बेकरार।
छोड़ के भीगी सी यादें,
कहता ये अलविदा सावन है।
कहता ये अलविदा सावन है।

34. पर सब चंदू कहते थे उसे

नन्हे हाथों में कलम न थी,
और न किताब थी मिली उसे।
कुछ सिक्कों की लालच ने,
उसका बचपन बर्बाद किया।
कभी सड़कों पे फैलाए हाथ,
कालिख में लिपटे एक कल का साथ।
कहीं दोपहर की धूप में वो,
कुछ जूतों को चमकाता था।

फिर रात की काली चादर तले,
किसी सेठ को चाय पिलाता था।
नाम पता कुछ खबर नहीं,
पर सब चंदू कहते थे उसे।
पर सब चंदू कहते थे उसे।

जब उमर थे स्वर व्यंजन के,
तो हुआ सामना गलियों से।
जब जाते थे स्कूल सभी,
देखे उन्हें घर की जालियों से।
सरकार से भी उम्मीद क्या करता,
थे फ़िज़ूल के उनके वादे।

अक्षरों से न तो हुयी दोस्ती,
पर उसके थे ऊंचे इरादे।
उसके सपनों की भनक नहीं,
पर सब चंदू कहते थे उसे।
पर सब चंदू कहते थे उसे।

करता था काम किसी सेठ के घर पे।
दो वक़्त का खाना मिलता था।
कुछ फटे पुराने कपड़ों में,
उसका हर हफ़्ता कटता था।
इक बार जो चोरी हुयी थी घर में,
उस सेठ ने उसकी रपट लिखाई।
फिर बंद किया उसे थाने में,
न फिर हुयी कभी उसकी रिहाई।

ठप हो गया बचपन उसका,
सड़ गयी जवानी जेल में ही।
बनके गुनाहगार वो निकला,
अपने जीवन के खेल में ही।
अगर वो मुजरिम न बनता,
तो क्या बनता वो पता नहीं।
पर सब चंदू कहते थे उसे।
पर सब चंदू कहते थे उसे।

35. आज का नेता

वो है नेता इस भारत का।
वो है नेता इस भारत का।
सत्ता के खेल में ईंट है वो,
गठ-जोड़ की नयी इमारत का।
क्रिकेट से मिली फ़रारी है।
पर उसके पास सफ़ारी है।
पर इन सब से पीछे हैं हम,
न अपनी कोई सवारी है।
जो ये होटल में खाऐं तो,
चालिस पन्नों का कार्ड मिले।
ये जब निकलें कभी दौरे पर,
रहते अलर्ट सारे जिले।
देख के सड़कों पे गड्ढे,
इनके आंसू न गिरते हैं।
पर वोट-बैंक के नाम पे ये,
पब्लिक के पीछे दिखते हैं।
फ़ेसबुक पे भी अप्डेट मिले,
और ट्विटर पे मिलते इनके ट्वीट।
घपलों में जब ये फ़सते हैं,
इनकी आपस में होती मीट।
कोर्ट से बचने की खातिर,
ये कहते हैं फ़िर राष्ट्रपति से,
एक आर्डिनेन्स तो पास करो।
हमको बचना है दुर्गति से।

ये चुनाव जब जीतें तो,
हम अक्सर पछताते हैं।
इनको फ़िर अब न सीट मिले,
हम फ़िर से यही मनाते हैं।

36. ठहराव के आगे

क्यों मैं सोचूं कि अब मेरी,
पहचान ख़तम होती है दिखी?
क्यों मैं सोचूं कि दुनिया ने,
है मेरी भी तकदीर लिखी?
इस अन्धकार सी नगरी में,
क्यों ये कदम न टिकते हैं।
जिनसे दिखी थी राहें मुझे,
क्यों वो चिराग न दीखते हैं।

      न पता कि अब इस राह को भी,
      फिर कौन सी करवट लेनी है।
      न पता कि उगते सूरज को,
      फिर कब दस्तक देनी है।
      ये किस जहां में पहुंचा हूँ,
      ये सोच के हूँ हैरान सदा।
      देख के नाकामी सूरत,
      किस सोच में है फिर सारा जहां?

किस से पूछूं कि अब मुझको,
आगे किस और को जाना है?
जिसने मुझे फिर यहाँ रोका है,
नाकामी का ही वो बहाना है।

      जो मिले अब रौशन कारवाँ,
      एक नयी सुबह को चाहूँगा।
      आगे बढ़ने की जो सोची तो,
      अपनी हर मंज़िल पाऊंगा।
      जिस और है जाना तय किया,

उस ओर ही अब मैं जाऊँगा।

37. इंतज़ार है उस दिन का

है अन्धकार से भरा आसमां,
दिखती न सुबह की लाली है।
टिम टिम करते तारे फिर भी,
रात की चादर काली है।

थक हार के फिर मैं बैठ गया,
और सुबह की राह भी ताकूँ मैं।
पलकें अब चुप हैं सोच के कि,
सुबह न आने वाली है।

लेकिन ये तोड़ेंगी खामोशी,
क्योंकि इन्हें सबकुछ कहना है।
कब अर्ज़ ये बातों को,
इंतज़ार है उस दिन का।
हाँ, इंतज़ार है उस दिन का।

आगे बढ़ने से पहले भी,
था कुछ लोगों का साथ मिला।
पर संग मेरे न चल सके,
ऐसा था उनका काफ़िला।

था उन्हें आगे चलना फिर भी,
संग चलने की गुज़ारिश की,
सब की मंज़िल पर एक न थी।
टूटा फिर साथ का सिलसिला।

लेकिन मैं ज्यादा दूर नहीं,
कुछ दूर ही अब तो चलना है।

कब फतह करूँ मंजिल अपनी,
इंतज़ार है उस दिन का।
अब इंतज़ार है उस दिन का।

38. ये उमीदें हैं आस मेरी

हर माँ बाप का सपना होता है की उनका लड़का आने वाले कल में उनका नाम रौशन करेगा। ये सपना उसके पैदा होते ही उससे जुड़ जाता है। धीरे धीरे ये उमीदों का रूप लेते हैं।

ये कविता एक ऐसे परिवार को प्रदर्शित करती है जिसका एकलौता लड़का अपने बाप का सहारा होता है। उस गरीब परिवार की उमीदें उससे जुडी हुयी थी। पर जब उस युवक का सपना सच होने का समय आता है, तब उसके पिताजी ज़िंदगी की आखिरी साँसें गिन रहे होते हैं। और उस युवक की प्रार्थना रहती है की जो सपने इतने सालों बाद सच हुए हैं उनको देखने के लिए उसके पिता को कुछ और साँसों की मोहलत मिल जाए।

❧❧❧

आँखों में तेरे हैं सपने,
पर साथ में कुछ मजबूरी है।
उन सपनों की भी है कीमत,
बिन उनके रात अधूरी है।
जो आज है तेरी अन्धकार से,
लथपथ एक कहानी ये,
क्यों छोड़ेगा तू उमीदें?
ये उमीदें हैं आस मेरी।
ये उमीदें हैं आस मेरी।

जो आज नहीं मैं कुछ भी हूँ,
कल होगी एक पहचान मेरी।
तेरा अंधियारा दूर करे,
होगी एक ऐसी शान मेरी।

देकर इन आँखों में सपने,
क्यों मुझे अलविदा कहता तू!
ये सब तो एक विरासत है,
जो रहती हैं अब पास मेरी।
जो रहती हैं अब पास मेरी।

बचपन में तेरा था आसरा,
माँ ने भी मुझे दुलारा था।
तब से मैं तेरे इस कल का,
इकलौता नया सहारा था।
जो कल की सुबह आनी है,
वो सब तेरी बदौलत है।
जो साथ नहीं तू इस कल में,
ये सुबह भी है उदास मेरी।

39. अपने मकसद पे अड़ते हैं

जिस देश की नींव रखी उसने,
दी जिसने क्रांति की परिभाषा,
उस देश पे मिटने वालों में,
दिखती नहीं कल की अभिलाषा।
क्या वजह है कि वो कहते हैं,
"इस देश में अब कुछ रहा नहीं"?
जब लुटने लगी थी आबरू,
क्यों किसी ने कुछ भी कहा नहीं।

चुप खड़े हैं सब ये सोचते हैं,
कि बाकी क्यों चुप रहते है।
जब बात उठे इल्ज़ामों की,
अगले को दोषी कहते हैं।
होकर उस कल पे न्योछावर,
लिखी जिन्होंने नयी कहानी,
ये देख निराशा उन्हें मिली,
कि व्यर्थ गयी हर कुर्बानी।
किस बात है अब अकड़ बची,
सब कुछ तो अपना बिखर गया।
हम सोच के फिर क्यों रोते हैं,
कल का हर सपना किधर गया।

थी जिनके लिए ये कुर्बानी,
वो खुद में अक्सर लड़ते हैं।
जब बात उठे इस देश की फिर,
मतलब की सोच में सड़ते हैं।

जनहित से पहले अपना हित,
ये उसूल अब दिखता है।
है जिसको अधिकार मिला,
वो इतिहास को लिखता है।
ये उसूल भी बदलेगा,
जब नयी सोच का वस्त्र मिले।
अपना ये कल फिर संवरेगा।
जब अधिकारों का अस्त्र मिले।

संग मिलकर कल की सुबह की,
सोच में अब हम पड़ते हैं।
लेकर अधिकारों का तर्कश,
अपने मकसद पे अड़ते हैं।

40. फिर भी उस राह पे चलता हूँ

शायद मैं कहीं भटक रहा था।
शायद कहीं और निकल चला था।
मैं मीलों आगे पहुँच गया,
रस्ता तो मेरा वहीँ खड़ा था।
ठहरा न लम्हा हाथों में,
न वक़्त था कि मैं मुड़ सकूँ।
वापस ढूढुं उस रस्ते को,
जिस रस्ते से फिर जुड़ सकूँ।

फिर भूल के मैं उस मंज़िल को,
मैं नयी राह अब चुनता हूँ।
एक नयी राह अब चलता हूँ।
ये सोच के आगे बढ़ा था मैं,
कि न होगी अब हार मेरी,
पर आगे थी जो मुश्किलें,
उनसे ही थी यलगार मेरी।

उम्मीद जो मन में बाकी थी,
उसने अपनी एक राह चुनी।
मैंने लाख मनाया पर,
फिर भी न उसने मेरी सुनी।
न है हिसाब क्या खोया मैं,
फिर भी उस राह पे चलता हूँ।
फिर भी उस राह पे चलता हूँ।

41. ये ज़िन्दगी की दौलतें

है कुछ लम्हों की ज़िन्दगी,
फिर भी बुनें हम ख्वाब क्यों?
कितनी है दौलत अब बची,
ढूढें हम इसका जवाब क्यों?
मेरे बुने इन ख़्वाबों से,
जो कल मुझे मिल भी गया,
मिल कर कभी जो खो सके,
चाहूँ मैं ऐसा सवाब क्यों?

ये ज़िन्दगी की दौलतें,
कुछ रोज़ की हैं अब बची।
कुछ रोज़ की हैं अब बची।
था नासमझ मैं भी तो इतना,
कि न हुआ एहसास ये,
थोड़े बचे इस वक़्त में,
कहीं खो न दूँ जो ख़ास है।
जो पल जिए खोने के डर से,
वो तो कब के गुज़र गए।
पर खोने का डर जो मिला,
अब तक वो मेरे पास है।

जो साँसों की हैं मोहलतें,
कुछ रोज़ तक ही हैं मिली।
कुछ रोज़ तक ही हैं मिली।

42. एक ठहराव जरूरी है

तू रुका है पर टूटा तो नहीं।
था साथ जो कल छूटा तो नहीं।
तेरी कोशिश से खुश हैं सभी,
तुझसे है कोई रूठा तो नहीं।
आगे बढ़ने के लिए भी,
एक ठहराव जरूरी है।
एक ठहराव जरूरी है।

रहता नहीं सबकुछ पहले सा,
हर पल भी कभी टिकता ही नहीं।
जो अभी है तारा अम्बर का,
वो सुबह में तो दिखता ही नहीं।
एक नयी सुबह के लिए भी,
एक बदलाव जरूरी है।
एक बदलाव जरूरी है।

हैं मुश्किलें राहों में कई,
तुझे उनसे है लड़ना भी अभी।
रस्ता देखे मंजिल तेरा,
जहां पहुचेगा तू भी तो कभी।
अपनी जीत पाने के लिए,
एक टकराव जरूरी है।
एक टकराव जरूरी है।

43. वो चला जा रहा है

रिश्ते नातों को कफ़न दिए,
अरमानों को दफ़न किये,
वो चला जा रहा है।
वो चला जा रहा है।

भूल के वो सबकी बातें,
करके अनसुनी कुछ फरियादें,
देकर आंसू इन आँखों में,
जो यार था मेरा लाखों में,
ओझल हो गया वो नज़रों से।
न पता मिला फिर खबरों से।

समेट के सारे सपनों को,
भूल के सारे अपनों को,
वो चला जा रहा है।
वो चला जा रहा है।

44. एक तू ही है मेरा हमसफ़र

गिरते संभलते,
यूं ही चलते चलते,
तूने है जीना सिखा दिया।
राहों में मेरे,
थे जब भी अँधेरे,
तूने है रस्ता दिखा दिया।
एक तू ही है मेरा हमसफ़र।
एक तू ही है मेरा हमसफ़र।

चलने से पहले पूछा जो खुद से,
"क्यों है तू अकेला राहों में"
फिर तेरी पनाहें मुझे मिली।
तूने है थामा फिर बाहों में।

मुश्किलों का जैसे है एक समंदर,
न दिखता है मुझे अब किनारा।
बस एक तुझपे है मुझे भरोसा।
बस एक तेरा ही है सहारा।
तुझको मैं चाहूँ हर एक सहर।
एक तू ही है मेरा हमसफ़र।

45. तब मैंने हथियार चुना

आवाज़ उठी जो सही के लिए,
हुकूमतों ने दफ़न किया।
उठ गया भरोसा वादों से ,
जिनका उन सब ने गबन किया।

कुछ सन्नाटों में चीखें थी,
जिनको किसी ने भी न सुना।
फरियादें जब हुयी अनसुनी,
तब मैंने हथियार चुना।

एक सुनहरे कल का ख्वाब जो देखा,
इस दिल में कई उमीदें थी।
एक नयी सोच से सजी हुयी,
मेरी आँखों की नीदें थी।

बिखर गया ख्वाबों का जहां,
जिसको सदियों से मैंने बुना।
जब राख हुयी सब उमीदें,
तब मैंने हथियार चुना।

46. कब दूर ये बेनूरी होगी

न दिखता है रस्ता कोई,
धुंधला सा यहाँ सवेरा है।
है दिशा कहाँ मुझको न पता,
ये कहाँ कारवाँ मेरा है।

एक रौशनी की है तलाश,
कब ये तलाश पूरी होगी।
कब बीतेगी ये रात अँधेरी,
कब दूर ये बेनूरी होगी।

हो घना अँधेरा कितना भी,
छटता है सुबह के होने पे।
रौशनी का एक ज़र्रा भी,
आता है रात के सोने पे।

मेरी मंज़िल भी दूर है मुझसे,
कब ख़फ़ा भी ये दूरी होगी।
कब बीतेगी ये रात अँधेरी,
कब दूर ये बेनूरी होगी।

47. एक परिंदा अब न रहा

एक परिंदा अब न रहा।
एक परिंदा अब न रहा।
जिसने देखे थे ख्वाब कई,
जिसकी यादें पीछे रह गयी।
जो खुला आसमां समझ के उसने,
अपनी एक परवाज़ चुनी,

टूट गए अरमां उसके,
न किसी ने उसकी आह सुनी।
उड़ न सका है वो फिर कभी,
जबसे सपने कुर्बान हुए।
ख्वाब थे जितने आँखों में,
सब उससे अन्जान हुए।

एक परिंदा अब न रहा।
एक परिंदा अब न रहा।
जिसने दी सबको सोच नयी,
जिसकी यादें कुछ कह गयी।
नयी सुबह और नया हो कल,
ऐसे कुछ उसके सपने थे।
न थे उससे नाते रिश्ते,
फिर भी सब उसके अपने थे।

पूरे हों अरमान उसके,
ऐसा दिन कभी न आया था
सबको खुशियाँ बांटी उसने,
बदले में कुछ नहीं पाया था।

उस एक परिंदे की परवाज़ें,

याद सभी को आती हैं।
वो सोच कभी न रुक पाए।
सदियाँ ये सबक भी पाती हैं।

48. एक नयी सुबह को करें सलाम

उन बातों को हम भूल गए,
जिन बातों से तकरार बढ़ी।
उन दीवारों को तोड़ गए,
जो सबके थी बीच खड़ी ।
कब तक रखें उन बातों को,
छुपा के अपने दिल में हम,
जिनसे हम कोसों दूर रहे,
जिसने की सबकी आँखें नम!

क्या खोया सब भूल के हम,
लें एक दूजे की बाहें थाम।
भुला के सारी नफरत को,
एक नयी सुबह को करें सलाम।

जो लड़े कभी हम मजहब पे,
एक दूजे का खून बहा।
धरती रोई फिर सदियों तक,
कल जो ये लहू लुहान रहा।
जो पास थी अपने वो दौलत,
उसकी न हमको कदर रही।
उनसे हम दिलों को जीत सकें,
ऐसी न हमको खबर रही।

ढूढ़ के लायें वो दौलत,
चाहो हो जो भी अंजाम।
भुला के सारी नफरत को,
एक नयी सुबह को करें सलाम।

49. जब कभी यहाँ अँधेरे हों

जो तेरी किरणें पड़ती हैं,
तो धरती अपनी है उजली।
दूर से ही आकाश दिखे,
शाम भी न रहती धुंधली।
शाम की घूंघट न रहती,
तुझसे जब यहाँ सवेरे हों।
तुझसे ही पथ उजियारे हों,
जब कभी यहाँ अँधेरे हों।

तुझसे जलती दीपक अपनी,
जब कभी यहाँ अंधियारा हो।
गर्व हो सूरज को तुझसे,

तुझसे रौशन घर सारा है।
सबके चूल्हे जलते तुझसे,
तुझसे मंडप में फेरे हों।
तुझसे ही पथ उजियारे हों,
जब कभी यहाँ अँधेरे हों।

तुझको नहीं कोई छू पाए,
तेरा कोई आकार नहीं।
तू तो है अनमोल सदा,
तेरा कोई व्यापार नहीं।
तुझसे धरती पे अन्न उगे,
जब कभी ये बादल घेरे हों।
तुझसे ही पथ उजियारे हों,
जब कभी यहाँ अँधेरे हों।

50. जंग न उनपे लग जाए

जिस धड़कन में बहती थी कभी,
एक सोच वो क्रांति को लाने की,
उसको है अब जंग लगी,
उसकी है घड़ी थम जाने की।

हम कोसते हैं उस गद्दी को,
जिसपे बैठे हैं भ्रष्ट सभी,
जिनके वादे भी अधूरे हैं,
पूरे न होंगे वो भी कभी।

हैं उम्मीदें उनसे ही जुड़ी,
जो बदलें नींव जमाने की।
हैं उनकी ही कोशिश पे टिकी,
एक सोच सुबह को लाने की।
बारूद हैं जिन विचारों विचारों में,
जंग न उनपे लग जाए।
जंग न उनपे लग जाए।

कुछ सोचते हैं धन दौलत की,
कुछ भागते हैं कल के पीछे।
कर्म की सीढ़ी छोड़ के सब,
क्यों भागते हैं फल के पीछे।
न फ़ुरसत है उनको भी अभी,
कि याद करें कुर्बानी वो,
जिसने सींचा इस धरती को,
जिनकी है एक निशानी वो।

उन कुर्बानियों को भूल गए,
एक होड़ में आगे जाने की।

अब उन्ही से होगा रौशन कल,
जो सोचें क्रांति को लाने की।
बारूद हैं जिन बंदूकों में,
जंग न उनपे लग जाए।
जंग न उनपे लग जाए।

51. कुछ राहें थी ऐसी मिली

कुछ राहें थी ऐसी मिली,
जिनसे जुडी थी शोहरतें।
उन शोहरतों से मैं जुड़ूं,
ऐसी थी मेरी हसरतें।
उन राहों पे जो चल पड़े,
कुछ राहें पीछे रह गयी।

न थम सके विश्वास मेरा,
ऐसा फ़साना कह गयी।

कुछ कर गुजरने की लहर,
जो थी मेरे मन में उठी,
नाकामी और एक हार थी,
जो वक़्त के संग बाह गयी।

उन शोहरतों पे मैं खड़ा,
मेरी नयी पहचान है।
जिसकी है मुझसे,
उसके लिए ये शान है।

वो राहें थी कुछ कह गयी।
और कुछ सबक भी दे गयी।
पर राहों की जो अहमत,
उनसे सभी अंजान हैं।

52. दर्द का है कारवाँ

दर्द की है एक ज़ुबाँ,
ये बहुत कुछ बोलती।
अपनी है पहचान क्या,
राज़ भी ये खोलती।
सामने तो है खड़ा,
एक खुला सा आसमां।
पर यहाँ उड़ने से पहले
दर्द का है कारवाँ।

देख के रौशन जहां,
मैं भी तो था खुश कभी।
गुम हुयी वो रौशनी,
हूँ जिसे ढूढता मैं अभी।
है सामने मेरे बसा
एक वो रौशन सा जहां।
पर यहाँ जुड़ने से पहले,
दर्द का है कारवाँ।

न यहाँ मैं जानता,
कि क्या मेरी पहचान है।
शाख से जैसे गिरे,
पत्ते की ना कोई शान है।
बन के गुल मैं खिल सकूँ
है कहाँ वो बागबां
ख़त्म हो जाकर जहां
जो दर्द का है कारवाँ

53. बस तेरा ही होना चाहूँ

है आसमा, तुझसे ये इबादत,
तारो के संग हो अपनी शोहबत।
तू ऐसी ख्वाइश है मेरी,
तू बन चूका है मेरी शिद्दत।
आकर मैं तेरी पनाहों में,
तारों सा जुड़ना चाहूँ।
हो तुझमें ही मेरा ये बसेरा,
बस इतना मैं तुझसे चाहूँ।

सावन के आने से तू
बादलों में यूँ छिप जाता है।
आफताब तेरे माथे का
इनमे ही कहीं खो जाता है।
इन बादलों के पीछे मैं,
तुझमे ही दिखना चाहूँ।
उस चंदा से तू मुझे मिला,
साथी उसका बनना चाहूँ।

रात की काली चादर में
तू गुम है कहाँ न जानू मैं।
इमारतों के पीछे है छुपा,
ऐसा ही अब मानू मैं।
तू है कितना दूर खड़ा,
ये दूरी कम करना चाहूँ।
थाम लू तेरे आँचल को,
बस तेरा ही होना चाहूँ।

54. वो वीर सपूत थे भारत के

पश्चिम का ही परचम था।
उम्मीद का दीपक मद्धम था।
जो गीत रचे नए कल के
आज़ादी का ही सरगम था।
खुदगर्ज़ नहीं वो रहा कभी,
जब आहुति देनी पड़ी।
अपने लहू से सींची धरती,
जिसपे है आज की नींव खड़ी।
थी जिनके रग में कुर्बानी,
थी जिन्होंने आज़ादी की ठानी,
वो वीर सपूत थे भारत के
वो वीर सपूत थे भारत के।

बातों का भी दौर चला।
सत्याग्रह कुछ दिन और चला।
उनकी आंखों में जाने कब से,
एक नयी सुबह का ख़्वाब पला।
हांथ सने बारूदों से,
सीने में भी चिंगारी थी।
बेड़ियों को तोड़ने की
उनकी कवायद जारी थी।
बात विचार जो विफल हुए,
संग्राम की अब तैयारी थी।
जो रहे सदा ही निगेहबान,
थामी रण की जिसने कमान,
वो वीर सपूत थे भारत के।

वो वीर सपूत थे भारत के।

जो रास न आया प्रेम भाव,
अब उन्होंने हुंकार भरी।
जा टकराए उस हुकूमत से,
जो रही सदा अहंकार भरी।

लाठी चली, गोली चली।
फांसी का डर भी बिसर गया।
कांप उठा अब दुश्मन भी,
सुनकर गरज ललकार भरी।

जिनसे है आबाद वतन,
जिनको है सबका नमन,
थे वीर सपूत वो भारत के।
हां वीर सपूत वो भारत के।

55. सरहद पे खड़ा सिपाही है

सबके मन में खुशहाली है, जब कदम टिके हैं रेतों में,
निगेहबान सरहद पे वो तो, है हरियाली खेतों में।
तिरंगे की वो आन बचाता, आज़ाद हिंद का राही है,
धरती अपनी महफ़ूज़ सदा जब, सरहद पे खड़ा सिपाही है।
बर्फ जमी है धरती पे, फिर भी वो कदम न हिलते हैं,
दुश्मन को जब मार गिराएं, तभी वो चेहरे खिलते हैं।
दोस्त तो पीछे छूट गया, दुश्मन तो अक्सर मिलते हैं,
घर की खुशियों में है दरार, वादों से जिनको सिलते हैं।
खून गिरे जो धरती पे, दुश्मन से डरता ना ही वो,
धरती अपनी महफ़ूज़ सदा जब, सरहद पे खड़ा सिपाही है।
घर से ख़त जो मिले उसे, आँखें उसकी नम होती हैं,
निगेहबान फिर भी है वो, आँखें न उसकी सोती हैं।
होकर शहीद जब घर पहुँचे, सबकी आँखें फिर रोती हैं,
सदियाँ भी क्यों न हों उदास, जब वो संताने खोती हैं।
जो अपने लहू से वतन को सींचे, सरफ़रोश की वो गवाही है।
धरती अपनी महफ़ूज़ सदा जब, सरहद पे खड़ा सिपाही है।

56. क्यों पीछे मुड़ कर देखूं

अपने कदम हैं राहों में,
मंज़िल पे हमें पहुचना है।
पथरीली हैं राहें तो क्या,
हैं राहों में कांटे तो क्या,
आगे है मंज़िल मेरी।
आगे चलने की मैं सोचूं।
क्यों पीछे मुड़ कर देखूं!

कुछ पीछे मैं छोड़ चला,
याद नहीं वो क्या था भला।
ठंडी छाओं ने मुह मोड़ा,
जब तपती धुप में रहा जला।
मंज़िल मेरी है दूर अभी,
रुकने की सोचूं और कभी।
क्यों थमने की मैं सोचूं?
क्यों पीछे मुड़ कर देखूं?

साथ में मेरे हैं सपने
और थोड़ी उम्मीदें हैं।
जगा रहूँ मैं रातों में,
न आँखों में नीदें हैं।
जब मंज़िल मिल जायेगी,
नींद तभी तो आएगी ।
मैं मंज़िल की ओर चलूँ,
क्यों पीछे मुड़ कर देखूं ।

57. साथ में जो ये ख्वाब रहें

साथ में जो ये ख्वाब रहें

वो दिन थे पढ़ने के जब,
ख्वाबों को साथ में लाया था
इनमें से कुछ घर से मिले,
कुछ दीवारों पे सज़ा के आया था।
ख्वाबों के बिन क्या जीना है,
ख्वाबों की मारामारी है
साथ में जो ये ख्वाब रहें,
मेरी ये दुनिया सारी है।

ख्वाबों का भी क्या कहना,
ये साथ चले ही आते हैं,
मंज़िल जो मिल जाए तो,
ये दूर कहीं चले जाते हैं।
बिन ख्वाबों के अब तो मेरा
जीना बहुत ही भारी है,
साथ में जो ये ख्वाब रहें,
मेरी ये दुनिया सारी है।

कुछ पन्नों पे नज़र पड़ी,
फिर मंज़िल कि ओर चला।
राह में आया मैखाना,
क्या करता मैं और भला।
बिखरे पन्नों की थी जो,
वो धुल गयी शराबों में,
कहाँ खो गए ख्वाब ये मेरे,
खोजूं मैं तुझे जवाबों में।
जिसने खोए इन ख्वाबों को,
वो रह गया भिखारी है,
साथ हैं जिनके ख्वाब हमेशा,
ऊनपे नज़र हमारी है.
साथ में जो ये ख्वाब रहें,
मेरी ये दुनिया सारी है।

58. उनकी खुशियों पे मरता हूँ

उनके ही हाथों में मैंने,
अपनी दो आँखें खोली थी।
साथ में उनके कुछ सपने थे,
और ममता कि झोली थी।
उनसे ही थी मेरी दिवाली,
और उनसे ही होली थी।
भले ही मुझसे कुछ न कहा,
पर आँखों में एक बोली थी।

वो मेरे भगवान् हैं और मैं,
उन्ही कि पूजा करता हूँ।
उन्ही के सपनो से जिंदा मैं,
उनकी खुशियों पे मरता हूँ।

दूर जो घर से मैं जाता हूँ,
वो आँखें नहीं सोती हैं।
मैं जब मुश्किल में पड़ जाऊं,
फिर वो आँखें रोती हैं।
घर वापस फिर कब आएगा,
उनसे यही बातें होती हैं।

उनके सपने साकार करूँ,
यही मैं सोचा करता हूँ।
उन्ही के सपनो से जिंदा मैं,
उनकी खुशियों पे मरता हूँ।

दूर भले में उनसे हूँ,
पर सपनों से नज़दीक हूँ मैं।
साथ जो मेरे उनकी दुआएं,

फिर तो यहाँ पे ठीक हूँ मैं।
ख़ुशी तो है मंजिल पाने कि,
साथ में दूरी का है ग़म ।

उनके ख़त जो मिले मुझे तो,
आँखें मेरी होती हैं नम।
किस हाल में हैं वो पता नहीं,
उनकी परवाह मैं करता हूँ।
उन्ही के सपनो से जिंदा मैं,
उनकी खुशियों पे मरता हूँ।

59. इसी बात से डरता है

मुझको अब किस ओर है जाना,
ये कुछ नहीं समझता है।
जब कोई मुश्किल आये तो,
दिल ये मेरा उलझता है।
      रास्ते तो कई हैं लेकिन,
      मंज़िल कि कुछ पहचान नहीं।
      उन्ही रास्तों पे चलना है,
      और कोई अरमान नहीं।
            ये दिल है नादान मेरा,
            हर बार ये गलती करता है।
            फिर ये गलती न कर बैठे,
            इसी बात से डरता है।

खुला आसमा देख के इसने,
ख्वाहिश राखी है उड़ने की।
देख के सबको साथ में उड़ते,
उनसे कोशिश है जुड़ने की।
      आसमा कि थाह नहीं,
      इस बात से ये अनजाना है।
      थक के वापस फिर आएगा,
      दिल को ये समझाना है।
            फिर से ख्वाहिश न कर बैठे,
            यही तो ख्वाहिश करता है।
            फिर ये गलती न कर बैठे,
            इसी बात से डरता है।

60. मेरी उड़ान

ख्वाहिशें कुछ ऐसी हैं,
कि आसमां में मैं उड़ जाऊं,
बादलों को मैं छू लूँ
और इन्द्रधनुष के रंग पाऊं।
आसमान में घर हो मेरा,
परिंदों संग हो वहाँ बसेरा।

उड़ती पतंगों से पूछुंगा
कि तेरी है डोर कहाँ।
आसमान से पूछूँगा मैं,
है तेरा ये छोर कहाँ।
दिन ढलने पर भटक न जाऊं,
इसी बात से डरता हूँ ।

फिर यही सोच कर मैं रह जाऊं,
कि ऐसी ख्वाहिश क्यों करता हूँ।
इस डर से मैं उड़ न पाऊं,
ना ऐसी मजबूरी है।
मंजिल को पाने के लिए,
अपनी तैयारी पूरी है।

61. मुझसा न महफ़ूज़ कोई

यह रचना, आज़ादी का अमृत महोत्सव की लोरी प्रतियोगिता में जिला स्तर पर (बरेली में) द्वितीय स्थान प्राप्त कर चुकी है।

❧❧❧

स हिम कि शीतल बाहों में,
गंगा जमुना कि राहों में,
पर्वत के फैले पहरों में,
गाँव, गली और शहरों में,
मुझसा न महफ़ूज़ कोई।

वो वीर जवानों कि कुर्बानी,
सौ सदियाँ जिनकी रहें दीवानी,
जब तोड़ा था ज़ंजीरों को,
और न चलने दी थी मनमानी,
जगती दिन रात निगाहों में,
इस स्वर्ग सी तेरी पनाहों में,
मुझसा न महफ़ूज़ कोई।

चंद्रशेखर, गांधी और भगत सिंह
जैसी जन्मी हस्ती जहां पे,
उस धरती को हर बार मैं चूमूं,
हर बार मैं चाहूँ जनम वहाँ पे।
मंदिर में और मीनारों में,
सेना कि खड़ी दीवारों में,
मुझसा न महफ़ूज़ कोई।

62. एक आज़ाद परिंदा हूँ

तिनके सा मेरा ये जहां,
उड़के मैं जाऊं और कहाँ।
तू है तो मेरा सब कुछ है,
तेरे साए में जिंदा हूँ।
इस खुले आसमाँ में जैसे,
एक आज़ाद परिंदा हूँ।

तेरे आगे मैं कुछ भी नहीं।
दुनिया ये तुझसे चलती है।
तेरी दुआएं साथ रहें तो,
मेरी ये खुशियाँ पलती हैं।
अपनी हर गुस्ताखी पर
मैं बेहद शर्मिंदा हूँ।
इस खुले आसमाँ में जैसे,
एक आज़ाद परिंदा हूँ।

शाम के ढलते मैं आ जाऊं,
यह मेरी कोशिश रहती है।
अपने पर मैं वहाँ पसारू,
जिस ओर हवा ये बहती है।
लौट के मैं जो न आ पाऊं,
तू ऐसे क्यों रोता है,
ऐसे जैसे कि कोई,
अपने किसी को खोता है।

बिछड़ के तुझसे मैं तुझे रुलाऊं,
ऐसा न मैं दरिंदा हूँ।
इस खुले आसमाँ में जैसे,

एक आज़ाद परिंदा हूँ।

63. हमें पता है

कहते हैं कि तन मन धन,
भारत माता को है अर्पण।
कितना सच है ये हमें पता है।
कितना सच है ये तुम्हे पता है।

हमने देखा एक नया भारत,
सन सत्तावन की कुर्बानी में।
देश की हमने लाज बचाई,
सरहद पे लड़े जवानी में।

कहते हैं अब हमपे न
कोई आँख उठाएगा।
संसद में बैठा हर कोई
देश की लाज बचाएगा।
कितना सच है ये हमें पता है।
कितना सच है ये तुम्हे पता है।

सबने की वर्षों मेहनत,
फिर संविधान बनाया था।
विद्वानों ने तब जाकर,
ये भ्रष्ट तंत्र दफनाया था।
कहते हैं भारत पे हम अब
प्रजा का राज चलाएंगे।
देश में साक्षरता और उन्नति
का हम दीप जलाएंगे।
कितना सच है ये हमें पता है।
कितना सच है ये तुम्हे पता है।

आधा पैसा वो खाते हैं,

फिर बाकी हम सब पाते हैं।
जांच भी बैठे तो ये सारे,
साफ़ बरी होके आते हैं।
"भ्रष्ट सभी यहीं बसते हैं",
कहके सब हमपे हसते हैं।
कहते हैं की न्याय मिलेगा,
प्रयास अभी भी जारी है।

बहुत हो गयी तानाशाही,
अब प्रजातंत्र की बारी बारी है।
कितना सच है ये हमें पता है।
कितना सच है ये तुम्हे पता है।

64. मेरी परछाई

मेरी मंजिल यहाँ नहीं है,
मुझे और भी आगे जाना है ।
मुझे यहाँ पे नहीं है रुकना,
न ये मेरा ठिकाना है ।
मुझे बहुत ही देर लगेगी,
तू चाहे तो अभी लौट जा ।
तू चाहे तो अभी लौट जा ।

बुरे वक़्त में साथ न कोई,
तू मेरे संग आई है ।
न तेरा कोई नाम पता,
तू तो बस एक परछाई है ।
मुश्किलें अभी और हैं बाकी ।
तू चाहे तो अभी लौट जा।
तू चाहे तो अभी लौट जा।

न तू मेरी मंजिल है,
और न ही तू मेरा कारवां ।
फिर क्यों मेरे साथ आ गया,
जब पता नहीं मैं चला कहाँ।
आगे क्या हो कुछ पता नहीं।
तू चाहे तो अभी लौट जा।
तू चाहे तो अभी लौट जा।

65. तेरा ये पुत्र आभारी है

मेरी वो माँ है जिसका,
हिम जैसा है मस्तक।
दूर से आती सूरज की किरणें,
उसपे देती हैं दस्तक।
तू देवी है हर मंदिर की।
तेरा पुत्र पुजारी है।
मुझपे फ़ैले तेरे आँचल का,
तेरा ये पुत्र आभारी है।

पावन गंगा की है सौगंध,
न तुझे कभी रोने देंगे।
तेरी रक्षा में जाग रहे,
पहरेदारों को न सोने देंगे।
तेरी जय जयकार करे,
वो शिक्षक या व्यापारी है।
मुझपे फ़ैले तेरे आँचल का,
तेरा ये पुत्र आभारी है।

तेरी मिट्टी में हम जन्मे,
हमको इस मिट्टी पे गर्व।
सजा के तुझको रखेंगे,
हो मेला या कोई पर्व।
तेरे कहने पे तत्पर हैं,
ये पुत्र तो आज्ञाकारी है।
मुझपे फ़ैले तेरे आँचल का,
तेरा ये पुत्र आभारी है।

तेरे चरणों में शीष झुकाऊं,

तेरी जयजयकार करूँ।
तेरी रक्षा में अस्त्र उठाऊं,
तेरे ही आँचल में मरूं।
तुझको हम आज़ाद करेंगे।
अब ये शपथ हमारी है।
मुझपे फ़ैले तेरे आँचल का,
तेरा ये पुत्र आभारी है।

66. गाँव शहर सब प्यासा है

गाँव शहर सब प्यासा है।
दिखती हर ओर निराशा है।
जब तू बरसे बिन रोके तो,
दिखती बस हरियाली है।
पुष्प पेड़ सब बड़े हो गए,
हर उपवन में माली है।
अब धरती उगलेगी सोना,
हम सब की यही आशा है।

तू हमसे जो रूठ गया,
तो ये धरती अब रोती है।
बच्चे तो खाते हैं लेकिन,
मां तो भूखी सोती है।
खेत भी हैं सूखे पड़े,
फ़िर क्यों तेरा तमाशा है।

इस बरस तो तू ऐसा बरसा,
अपना घर तो टूट गया।
पानी ही पानी दिखता है,
सब कुछ पीछे छूट गया।
क्या ये तेरा नया रूप है,
अपनी ये जिज्ञासा है।
गाँव शहर सब प्यासा है।
दिखती हर ओर निराशा है।

67. क्रांति की गूँज

अपनी धरती आज़ाद है और
हम आज़ाद मुल्क़ के वासी हैं।
अपने दिल में फिर क्यों पलती,
एक ग़म और उदासी है।

कहाँ गयी वो सोच जिसे,
हम आधारशिला कहलाते थे?
एक नयी सुबह की देख झलकियां,
अपना मन बहलाते थे।
कहते थे कि लड़ जायेंगे,
वो अस्सी या इक्यासी हैं।

क्रांति की धार को जंग न लगने देना।
ये तेरा हथियार है रही।
तोड़ दे इस चक्रव्यूह को,
ये क्रांति की गूँज है सिपाही।
इस भ्रष्ट तंत्र से मुक्ति पाने को,
कुछ और भी सदियां प्यासी हैं।

68. कुछ देर ठहर जा बचपन

माँ का आँचल थाम के मैंने,
तब था चलना सीखा।
घर की कुछ दीवारों पे,
था हमने सबकुछ लिखा।
कुछ देर ठहर जा बचपन।
कुछ देर ठहर जा बचपन।
लिखी हुई उन यादों से
मैं खुलकर ये पूछूंगा,
कि तू कब वापस आएगा
तू कब वापस आएगा ?

स्कूल के भारी बस्ते में,
किताब का वो पन्ना था।
उन्ही किताबों को पढ़के,
कल और आज ये बनना था।
कुछ देर ठहर जा बचपन।
कुछ देर ठहर जा बचपन।
उस किताब के पन्ने से,
फ़िर से आज ये पूछूंगा,
क्या मेरा कल भी संवारेगा ?

बड़ों के साथ में जब कभी,
मैं बाहर निकला करता था,
अपनी ज़िद पे न डांट पड़े,
इसी बात से डरता था।
कुछ देर ठहर जा बचपन।
कुछ देर ठहर जा बचपन।

डांट के उस डर से पूछूंगा,
जो अक्सर मैं सुनता था,
क्या अब मुझे रोक तू पायेगा ?

एक सन्देश

आशा है मेरे विचारों ने आप सभी को प्रभावित किया होगा। मेरे विचार यहीं समाप्त नहीं होंगे। बहुत ही जल्द नए विचारों को आपके सामने प्रस्तुत करूँगा।